Scaffolding THE ACADEMIC SUCCESS OF
Adolescent English Language Learners

A Pedagogy of Promise

Aída Walqui & Leo van Lier

WestEd.org

Printed in the United States of America.

ISBN: 978-0-914409-75-5

Library of Congress Control Number: 2006922979

The book cover and text paper is certified by the Forest Stewardship Council. The text
is printed on 30% recycled paper.

WestEd is a nonpartisan, nonprofit research, development, and service agency with more
than a dozen offices nationwide, from Massachusetts, Vermont, and Washington, DC, to
Georgia, Arizona, and California, with headquarters in San Francisco.

WestEd books and products are available through bookstores and online
booksellers. WestEd also publishes its books in a variety of electronic formats.

To order books from WestEd directly, call our Publications Center at 888-293-7833, or
visit us online at www.WestEd.org/resources.

For more information about WestEd:

Visit www.WestEd.org

Call 415-565-3000 or toll free 877-4-WestEd

Write WestEd, 730 Harrison Street, San Francisco, CA 94107-1242

Chief Executive Officer: Glen Harvey

Chief Program Officer: Sabrina Lane

Chief Development Officer:
Catherine Wolcott

Publications Manager: Danny S. Torres

Communications Specialist: Tanicia Bell

Editor: Lynn Murphy

Managing Editor: Joy Zimmerman

Design Director: Christian Holden

Graphic Designer: Fredrika Baer

Proofreaders: Joan D. Saunders,
Rosemary de la Torres

Indexer: Ken Hassman

Contents

List of Figures

PREFACE

This book is for all middle school and high school content area teachers who have English language learners in their classes — whether these classes are designed specifically for English learners or are mainstream content area classes in which perhaps a few or even only one or two students are not yet proficient in English. Upper-elementary teachers, too, will find relevant ideas for teaching disciplinary content while supporting their students who are English language learners.

We have written this book with a growing sense of urgency. In the 10 years from 1995 through 2005, the U.S. school population in grades K–12 grew by less than 3 percent while the population of English language learners increased by 56 percent (Batalova et al., 2007). For English language learners in high school, the odds of academic success are daunting: one-half of them fail their graduation tests, leaving school without a diploma and unprepared for the workforce (Hopstock and Stephenson, 2003). In the future, demographers project, English language learners will increasingly be students who were born and educated *exclusively* in the United States. In California, for example, by 2025, only 17 percent of English language learners are expected to be first-generation immigrants; 83 percent will come from families that have been in the United States for two or even three generations (Passel, 2006).

In the face of such sobering statistics, this book offers a future-oriented pedagogy, one that looks ahead to what students can become and that builds on the knowledge, beliefs, and values all students bring to school. We reject the idea that English language learners have less promise than others. What is true, however, is that they have much more to learn than do their English-proficient peers, and their teachers have much more to teach. Furthermore, it is not as though teachers can approach English language learners as a homogeneous group. These students' ethnic, linguistic, and cultural backgrounds span the globe. Academically, their backgrounds range from having had rigorous instruction in their native language to never having attended school. As English learners, their appropriation of this new language is equally diverse. Not surprisingly, according to a survey of 5,000 California teachers, most feel insufficiently prepared to serve these students well. In addition, those teachers who know the most about working effectively with English language learners are most likely to find shortcomings in the instructional programs designed for these students (Gándara, Maxwell-Jolly, and Driscoll, 2005).

We wrote this book to offer concrete examples of what we call Quality Teaching for English Learners (QTEL), a way of teaching that accelerates what teachers can teach and English language learners can learn. Across the country, including in the New York City, Austin, and San Diego school districts, QTEL staff members and author Aída Walqui, who developed the QTEL approach, have worked with districts, schools, and individual teachers to engage learners' promise and enhance teachers' expertise. In this book, we visit a few of these classrooms and experience students' on-the-ground learning. Through extended vignettes and transcribed dialogue, we show how teachers have learned to structure challenging and inviting learning opportunities, as well as showing what they do to support students' learning once the invitation has been accepted. We also describe how other teachers can create similar high-challenge learning opportunities and provide high-support instruction.

It is no accident that sociocultural learning theory guides these teachers' practice and the lessons we describe. The QTEL principles for working with English language learners reflect explicit cognitive and social learning theories about how people learn in general, as well as how they learn in a new language. In the first three chapters of this book, we take care to describe these theories and the crucial notion of scaffolding. We have been advised that these chapters might not appeal to teachers who are more in need of practical ideas than of theoretical discussions. We agree that practice must be central; however, we also keep in mind the famous remark by psychologist Kurt Lewin that there is nothing as practical as a good theory. Theory without practice is useless, but practice without theory can be dangerous.

Even in the more theoretical chapters we have included many examples from classroom practice, both from the QTEL work reported in this book and from other sources. We are confident that the book as a whole brings practice and theory together in comprehensible and responsible ways. It is, of course, possible to read the last three chapters first and then study the first three chapters for the theoretical background. More beneficial, perhaps, is to start reading at the beginning and check cross-references to other chapters as you go along. In that way, we hope, it will become clear why we call the QTEL approach a "pedagogy of promise."

This is a book for practitioners more than for academics, but it takes the decidedly academic stance that teaching is an intellectual as well as a social and emotional calling. As teachers, all of us develop our own expertise when we can reflect on the theory that underlies our teaching decisions, that may cause us to insist, for example, that English language learners must talk, talk, talk about what they are learning (don't miss chapters 1 and 3) or that classrooms where interaction is a constant are classrooms where learning emerges and takes root (see chapters 1 and 2).

Contributing to our arguments for theory-based teaching, author Leo van Lier draws on his background as linguist, sociocultural learning theorist, and university teacher of language teachers. In disclosing that the authors, Walqui and van Lier, are married to each other, we hope you will understand the pervasive commingling of authorial voices, and we apologize for suggesting perhaps too much about the topics that animate their dinner table conversation.

Acknowledgments

As authors of this book, we owe gratitude to many colleagues, in and out of WestEd. Among the teachers who generously offered their expertise and classrooms for observation, videotaping, interviews, and our learning, we thank Tony DeFazio, previously at International High School at La Guardia Community College in Queens, New York; Roza Ng at MS 131 in Manhattan; Stacia Crescenzi at Lanier High School in Austin, Texas; Alice Cohen at Ridgewood Intermediate in the Bronx, New York; and multiple other colleagues who were very accommodating and willing to share their own process of apprenticeship with educators nationwide. The teaching staffs at all the schools mentioned above and their inspiring and hard-working students deserve thanks and recognition for having carried on normally as we intruded into their classrooms with notebooks in hand and recording gear at the ready.

There is a special group of colleagues, the QTEL team in San Francisco, who have been supportive and critical friends over the last decade, constantly probing and enhancing understandings as the QTEL vision, tools, and processes described here were developed. With heartfelt recognition of their expertise and professionalism, they are Donna Gaarder, Leslie Hamburger, Alex Insaurralde, Nanette Koelsch, Mary Schmida, and Steven Weiss. Many thanks also to colleagues Echo Chen and Patricia Lopez-Hurtado for their support to the team, and to far-flung QTEL colleagues Pia Castilleja, Nicholas Catechis, and Rose Vilchez.

The WestEd leadership recognized over a decade ago the need to focus on the education of adolescent English language learners. This is an opportunity to appreciate their support for that work and the work of the QTEL team. Special thanks are due Chief Program Officer Gary Estes for his generous help and wise counsel.

A group of readers helped refine ideas and provided valuable feedback. We especially want to thank Guadalupe Valdés, Pauline Gibbons, Cindy Pease-Alvarez, Robert Linquanti, Candy McCarthy, and Laura Alvarez for their perspectives from the classroom, the university, and the field of teacher professional development.

Finally, every writer knows that without a fine editor, ideas on paper do not always capture the essence of what one intends. Lynn Murphy at WestEd corralled a manuscript of many parts and made it tighter and more direct. We owe her much gratitude for her hard work and expertise. We assume total responsibility for all remaining limitations and errors in the text.

A PEDAGOGY OF PROMISE

Across the United States, in virtually every school district, teachers work with students whose native or primary language is not English. Often, teachers have not been prepared to work with the wide range of ethnic, cultural, academic, and linguistic diversity that is increasingly common in their classrooms, especially among their students who are English language learners. Yet, English language learners, like all students, arrive in our classrooms with immense potential, strengths to build on, and dreams for their future. It is our job as education professionals to help them realize that potential and to provide them with the right learning opportunities so that they can address rigorous academic content *in a language they have yet to master.*

In this chapter we introduce our core argument about the kinds of learning opportunities that support a "pedagogy of promise," teaching that is oriented toward developing students' future potential. Based on the work of Russian psychologist Lev Vygotsky and others who recognized that learning happens in *advance* of development and with particular kinds of support, a future-oriented pedagogy enlists students' inborn drive to belong to social groups, to learn with and from others, and to develop. While this kind of teaching is beneficial for all young people, it is particularly important for English language learners.

Helping Students Become What They Are Not Yet

How does the co-construction of understanding demonstrate a pedagogy of promise?

The approach to the education of English language learners developed by the Quality Teaching for English Learners (QTEL) initiative and described in this book proposes first of all that building on these students' promise *requires* engaging them in intellectual challenge. Second, it recognizes that high challenge requires high support. The QTEL approach also reflects our strong belief that teachers build their own expertise, in similar ways as their students, through intellectual challenge that is appropriately supported in collegial interactions, with reflection, and through ample practice. In the pages that follow, we argue for theory-based practice and we provide clear examples of what it looks like to provide students with high levels of challenge along with high levels of support.

Consider, for example, a New York middle school ESL class where two girls from the Dominican Republic work as partners to understand a Robert Frost poem, "The Road Not Taken," with its famous couplet, "I took the one less traveled by/And that has made all the difference." Their task is to complete a double-entry journal: in one column they offer their ideas about the two roads in the poem, in the other they support their ideas with quotes from the text. As the students work together, in a classroom where their teacher has created a climate in which learners support each other and develop their intellectual stamina, these two accept with interest the linguistic and conceptual challenges of their task and build on each other's thinking:

Student 1: If he wouldn't take the road, like maybe he wouldn't be like the place that he was.

Student 2: In that moment?

Student 1: *(Nods)* He would like, in a whole different place.

Student 2: He would be in a different place?

Student 1: *(Nods)*

Student 2: If he wouldn't take that way, he would be in another place? He wouldn't be in that place right now?

Student 1: *(Nods)*

Student 2: You know, if he wouldn't...

Student 1: If he wouldn't have been in that place...

Student 2: No, if he...you're confusing...

Student 1: If he wasn't...if he didn't took one path—

Student 2: The path that he took, he wouldn't be that place.

Student 1: *(Nods)* If he didn't take that path...

Student 2: *(Writing)* "If he didn't take that path," hang on, "he wouldn't be in the same..." *(rolls eyes, confused)*

Student 1: He wouldn't be—

Student 2: *(Lighting up)* In the place that he is right now?

Student 1: *(Nods)* In the place that he is now.

Both girls finish writing the statement in their double-entry journals.

Student 1: *(Reading aloud the next line in the poem)* "I took the one less traveled by"

Both girls: *(Completing the line in unison)* "And that has made all the difference."

Student 2: Yeah...

Long pause

Student 1: If he didn't take that one, that would change his life.

(Cohen and Walqui, 2007)

Focused on constructing understanding, these students are patient with each other and themselves, using language to work out nascent ideas. Their promise as thinkers and language learners is palpable.

The Theoretical Foundations of Future-Oriented Pedagogy

In what ways does your teaching reflect sociolinguistics, cognitive psychology, and sociocultural learning theory?

The pedagogy advanced in this book weaves together ideas drawn from sociolinguistics, cognitive psychology, and sociocultural learning theory. A brief overview of these assumptions about language and learning highlights the themes that will be developed in later chapters and amplified with classroom examples.

From sociolinguistics comes the notion that language is primarily social — a tool that human beings use to get things accomplished in the real world. This is a seemingly self-evident proposition until it is contrasted with another common way of thinking about language, primarily as syntactic, lexical, and phonetic systems. We use those — and other — systems when we communicate, but they are not what we focus on as we engage in interactions with others. We request, disagree, praise, suggest, and carry out other verbal interactions in ways that successfully accomplish what we intend, in ways that are appropriate to the social moment. Understanding language, therefore, is primarily a matter of understanding actions (utterances) based on an understanding of the contexts in which they are expressed: who said what, what relationship the speakers have with each other, where the expression is uttered, when, for what purposes, using what perspective, intending what goals. As language users, we focus on the social role of language: action and communication. A focus on language form (e.g., grammar), while also important, is secondary.

From cognitive psychology, we build on the extensive research carried out to understand the nature of learning: the importance of building on prior knowledge, establishing relationships between and across ideas, and focusing learner attention on the processes of knowing — thinking about thinking. This last aspect, metacognition, is extremely important for second language acquisition because it helps English language learners take control of their own learning and decide what to do when they do not understand the text at hand, whether it is oral or written (Bransford, Brown, and Cocking, 2000).

From sociocultural theory we bring in the assumptions that learning, especially in the early stages, is essentially social in nature. Ideas are initially acquired in interaction with others and only later are they owned conceptually. Language interactions between teachers and students, and among students, play a pivotal role in mediating the construction of knowledge. Students are socialized into the academic practices of adults through invitations to engage in activity with others, by receiving models of how that engagement is enacted, and by being provided with the support and opportunity to practice and eventually "own," or appropriate, those practices. As James Lantolf explains,

> [D]espite the label "sociocultural" the theory is not a theory of the social or of the cultural aspects of human existence…it is, rather…a theory of mind that recognizes the central role that social relationships and culturally constructed artifacts play in organizing uniquely human forms of thinking. (Lantolf and Thorne, 2006, p. 1)

As we will see in the next section, sociocultural theory underlies and structures the learning and pedagogical framework presented here for working with English language learners. Almost by definition, sociocultural theory describes a pedagogy of promise, a way of teaching that anticipates student learning that is just on the horizon.

The QTEL Application of Sociocultural Learning Theory

How do tenets of sociocultural learning theory apply to the co-construction of understanding demonstrated above by the two students' reading of "The Road Not Taken"?

Lev Vygotsky developed the basis of sociocultural theory in the 1920s and 1930s. Although he died in 1932 at the early age of 37, much of his work was translated and published posthumously. Vygotsky's ideas influenced many researchers, who have built on his legacy to propose ways of better understanding how human beings learn and, thus, how they can be taught (see, for example, Cazden 1981; Cole, 1985; Lantolf and Thorne, 2006; Rogoff, 1995; van Lier, 2004). QTEL incorporates the following tenets of sociocultural learning theory in understanding how to affect teaching and learning:

- Development follows learning (therefore, teaching precedes development).

- Participation in activity is central in the development of knowledge.

- Participation in activity progresses from apprenticeship to appropriation, or from the social to the individual plane.

- Learning can be observed as changes in participation over time.

Development follows learning (therefore, teaching precedes development)

Many times we hear teachers say they can't teach a specific unit or lesson to their English language learners because "their English is not there yet."

The assumption seems to be that before students can learn concepts and skills, they need to know the related language — that language and content are two separate entities. This idea derives from traditional developmental psychology, which posits that learning can only be successful after the learner's relevant mental functions have already matured.

Instead, and in line with thinking first proposed by Vygotsky, we believe that learning truly happens only if it is ahead of development. In response to teachers' worries, we would say that development occurs precisely because teachers plan lessons beyond the students' ability to carry them out independently. The catch, of course, is that the lessons be deliberately designed to present high support along with high challenge. This support comes by way of teacher invitations that engage students' intrinsic motivation, that involve students in using new concepts and new language in meaningful contexts, and that provide students with the opportunity to develop their understanding in interactions with others, at least initially. In this view, deliberate, well-constructed teaching drives development.

Participation in activity is central in the development of knowledge
Students develop higher-order functions as they engage in activity that requires them to use language. Vygotsky emphasized the primacy of linguistic mediation in the development of higher mental processes; he contended that language is the main vehicle of thought and that all language use is dialogical, that is, based on social interaction.

Even when social speech is internalized as inner speech, it remains essentially dialogical and social and continues to have the function of supporting thinking. When we are faced with a difficult task that requires much thought and concentration, we will often make our inner speech overt, turning it into private speech that is audible, but not directed at anyone but ourselves. For example, we might overhear a learner struggling with algebraic functions engage in private speech: "Oops, that can't be right... Maybe I should start by making a function table...Ah, good! I see why that relationship is off." In this instance we see language and thought intimately interconnected as the learner attempts to marshal resources and control the task. Language, then, is an abstract tool that mediates all learning, in the way that physical tools mediate the conduct of physical tasks.

If social interaction is the basis for language and learning, as described above, the notion of consciousness (awareness of self and one's surroundings), the development of identity, and physical and mental skills and abilities all emerge from and in interaction. As Vygotsky puts it, "[H]uman learning presupposes a specific social nature and a process by which children grow into the intellectual life of those around them" (1978, p. 88). "[E]very function in the child's development appears twice, on two levels. First, on the social, and later on the psychologicial level; first between people as an interpsychological category, and then inside the child as an intrapsychological category" (1978, p. 128). Children internalize what they learn in social interactions not by "copying and pasting," but through a process of transformation involving appropriation and reconstruction. In Vygotsky's view of pedagogy, all knowledge arises in social activity, and all learning is co-constructed, with the learner transforming the social learning into psychological, or individual, learning over time. Such learning, Vygotsky suggests, takes place in a learner's *zone of proximal development*.

The zone of proximal development (ZPD) is the most recognized — almost emblematic — construct in Vygotsky's theory of learning. The most often quoted definition of ZPD describes learning that results from interaction with someone more accomplished than the learner:

> It is the distance between the actual developmental level as determined by independent problem solving and the level of potential development

as determined through problem solving under adult guidance or in collaboration with more capable peers. (Vygotsky, 1978, p. 86)

Vygotsky also recognized, however, that interactions between peers with essentially equal knowledge could also result in learning. Many researchers (e.g., Donato, 1994; Gibbons, 2002; Mercer, 1995; Rogoff, 1995) have further developed this idea of joint construction of knowledge among peers (for further discussion, see chapter 2).

For Vygotsky and other sociocultural theorists, "problem solving under adult guidance or in collaboration with...peers" does not refer to just any and all kinds of "assistance" or "helping." First, learning presupposes, quite precisely, initiative and agency on the part of the learners. While the teacher must set up tasks that invite learner agency (i.e., active involvement and the development of autonomy), it is the collaborative work of the learners that will show their ZPD, or level of development to come, and the kind of support that will result in learning. Most of this book consists of the fundamentals of working within such proximal contexts and in supporting learners' proximal abilities, or abilities that are just on the horizon.

Participation in activity progresses from apprenticeship to appropriation, or from the social to the individual plane

As learners engage in collaborative activity beyond their individual ability to perform, they apprentice the ways of "doing it right," in accordance with the patterns of behavior valued by their community. If the task is a history discussion of multiple points of view, for example, students will learn how to make a statement or claim from a given perspective and how to use documentary evidence to articulate the assumptions or warrants that support the claim. English language learners, since they will be carrying out the activity in a language they do not fully understand, initially may imitate, uncomfortably, the models the teacher has provided. As they move from claim to claim in a scaffolded activity and work together with peers, their understanding increases. Over time, students appropriate the ability to make claims from a historical character's perspective. Support is there as needed, and it is adjusted as the learners' needs change. What the support enables is a gradual owning of processes, ideas, and language. To paraphrase Vygotsky, what students can do with support today, they will be able to do alone tomorrow.

The fostering of autonomy is what all good teaching is about. The process starts with carefully designed and supported pedagogical activity that provides, over time, the continuity for learners to make proximal ideas, relationships, and higher-order activities their own, along with the language required to express them.

Learning can be observed as changes in participation over time
If we want to see whether English language learners have appropriated knowledge, then, ideally, we should observe how they engage in similar activity over time. In the example of the history discussion above, students would tentatively repeat phrases they heard the teacher model, perhaps even use a list of formulaic expressions the teacher may have given them (see figure 1).

Two weeks later, a similar interaction on a different historical topic should show the same students now more comfortably using ideas and language they had encountered before. Now, no supports are needed, and there is more fluency in students' expressions, although their participation is still hesitant. A month or two later, we should observe students who are comfortably making claims and are now apprenticing how to express other activities central to the discipline.

Figure I. Formulaic Expressions for Analyzing Historical Consequences

From the perspective of X, what were some of the consequences of Y?

Some of the benefits that resulted from Y for X include...

Do you claim any other advantages?

On the other hand, there were also disadvantages for X, for example ...

Do you claim any other disadvantages?

Can you justify with evidence that Z was a positive consequence
(a benefit for X)?

Can you justify with evidence that W had a negative impact on X?

Taken together, these tenets of sociocultural learning theory enable us to propose a pedagogy of promise, one that looks at students' academic futures as the deliberate development of potential built on what they bring to the class. Rather than just focusing on students' past performance and achievements (what they have or have not learned so far), a teacher's role shifts to creating enticing opportunities for students to interact around key disciplinary topics, through the mediation of emergent language skills (Ellis, 2006). Given the linguistic and academic diversity of a class, the teacher determines what learning experiences will allow all students in the class to operate in their zone of proximal development and provides the needed supports. Urie Bronfenbrenner, an ecological psychologist, recounts an anecdote in which Vygotsky's colleague A. N. Leont'ev compares in a similar vein the difference between Soviet and American psychologists' approaches to child development: "American researchers are constantly seeking to discover how the child came to be what he is; we in the USSR are striving to discover not how the child came to be what he is, but how he can become what he is not yet" (from a conversation between Leont'ev and Bronfenbrenner in 1977, reported in Bronfenbrenner 1979, p. 40). Instead, then, of testing students at a given point in time to see what they learned in the past, it is more revealing to observe students' participation in academic activity over time, to see how their potential is gradually realized.

Conclusion

The future for the increasing number of our students who are English language learners depends on an education that sees, appreciates, and engages their promise. The learning theory developed by Lev Vygotsky and others points us toward educational practices that can meet the promise of English language learners precisely because these practices are organized around promise — the zone of proximal development and the supports that enable learners to move toward abilities that are just on the horizon.

In the next chapter, we will begin to see how the kinds of supports, or "scaffolding," that teachers provide enable students to make optimal learning gains. Because notions of "scaffolding" have at times drifted from their theoretical (and meaningful) base, we will focus on the critical differences between, on the one hand, simply helping students complete tasks they cannot do independently and, on the other hand, the theoretical intent of scaffolding — to create the contexts and supports that allow students to interact in their zone of proximal development.

SCAFFOLDING REFRAMED

Over the past few decades the metaphor of "scaffolding" has become widely — but also imprecisely — used in education. A fresh look at the origins of this concept can be helpful if we are to use the power of scaffolding to transform teaching. Scaffolding refers both to a special, supportive way of interacting and to a temporary structure that assists learning. As both a process and a structure, scaffolding can be described as the pedagogical ways in which the zone of proximal development (ZPD) is established and in which the work within the ZPD is carried out. In this sense, scaffolding and the ZPD go together.

The Zone of Proximal Development and the Peekaboo Game

How do the dynamics of the peekaboo game relate to the ZPD?

Vygotsky first introduced the ZPD as an approach to intelligence testing. He argued that if the tester looked not only at what the child could do independently, but also at what the child could do with assistance, this would give more accurate information about what the child might be able to achieve in the future. Later, Vygotsky applied this idea to contexts of schooling and play, sometimes specifying the necessary participation of more capable others (e.g., parents, teachers) to support learning, but sometimes simply allowing natural social interaction to take place, as in his description of play:

> ...play also creates the zone of proximal development of the child. In play a child is always above his average age, above his daily behavior; in play it is as though he were a head taller than himself. (1976, p. 552)

While Vygotsky presented powerful arguments for the social nature of learning and backed them up with a substantial array of experimental studies, his writings on the ZPD, particularly its application to teaching, were cut short by his early death. Many would agree that his "ZPD concept was unfinished, underspecified, and...presented contradictory explanations...at various times" (Lantolf and Thorne, 2006, p. 268). Continuing research by others has refined and expanded Vygotsky's initial ideas about how to support creation of the ZPD and the collaborative process of working within it.

In particular, much research has focused on the notion of scaffolding, which today is so strongly associated with the ZPD that many people wrongly assume the concept was introduced by Vygotsky himself. In fact, scaffolding owes its origin and wide recognition to psychologist and education researcher Jerome Bruner (who wrote the introduction to the first English translation, in 1962, of Vygotsky's seminal *Thought and Language*). Bruner, with a team of colleagues, investigated interactions between six pairs of mothers and infants over a period of 10 months, especially in the game of peekaboo. The researchers analyzed what they called the mothers' opportunities to provide a "scaffold" for their infants' learning (Bruner and Sherwood, 1976).

Peekaboo

Imagine a mother and her baby. The mother engages the infant's attention and then suddenly covers her face with her hands and "disappears," to the consternation or even alarm of the infant. After a short while, the mother removes her hands from her face, says "Boo," and the baby, immensely relieved upon this miraculous return of the mother, coos in pure delight and waves her arms and legs enthusiastically. This is the peekaboo game, which apparently is played by mothers and infants all over the world, even though the word "boo" might be replaced by "piep-piep" (in Holland), "Ky Ky" (in Ukraine), "aca ta" (in Perú), and so on.

In looking closely at the dynamics of peekaboo, Bruner and his colleagues found that the game had a basic structure that was always the same (they called it the "syntax" of the game):

- establishing contact (mutual engagement or attention-focusing);

- disappearing (hiding, by other or child, of face, self, or toy);

- reappearing; and

- reestablishing contact.

In addition to these "obligatory" features that define the game, peekaboo had optional features, including vocalizations, gestures, and ways to hide (e.g., behind hands, a cloth, a chair, a wall). Together, the obligatory and optional elements form the "rule-bound" aspects, or *structure,* of the game (1976, p. 280).

Predicting the Unpredictable

The *structure* of the game is predictable: we know that initial engagement, contact, or joint attention will be established; we know that some hiding or disappearing will occur; and we also know that after a short while there will be a reappearing. On the other hand, the *process* of carrying out the game — the actual moment-to-moment words and actions that occur — is much less predictable: new developments may occur at any time on the initiative of either the mother or child or because of chance occurrences. Bruner and his colleague Virginia Sherwood introduce the term "scaffold" to capture the mother's responsiveness to the child's unexpected actions that occur in the process of the game:

> It is to [the child's] initiatives that the mother often responds with vocalizations as if to control the child's activation. This part of the game is characteristically "non-rule-bound" and seems to be an instance, rather, of the mother providing a scaffold for the child. (1976, p. 280)

The important thing to note here is that, in this first appearance of the term, the scaffolding occurs during the "non-rule-bound" parts of the game. In other words, at this point the structure ("syntax") of the game is not the scaffold. Nor is the game itself the scaffold. (Though, later on, when scaffolding is extended to the education context, the meaning of the term expands to include the planning and setting up of the task or activity.) As first conceived by Bruner and Sherwood, the scaffold happens *when new and unpredicted behaviors emerge,* such as vocalizations and movements, and it refers to the mother "control[ling] the child's activation." In addition to controlling, we may add channeling and stimulating the child's activation, even making it possible for the child to be a "head taller than himself," to use Vygotsky's phrase. The mother will take every sign of an emerging new skill (a word, a movement, an expression) as an opportunity to engage the child in higher-level functioning. So, for example, a vocalization will be interpreted as a meaningful utterance and will be responded to as such; a pointing gesture will be taken as a sign of expectation and may be responded to by delaying and then fulfilling the anticipated next action, and so on. Rather than controlling, scaffolding is the process of responding to the child's awakening sense of agency and, therefore, initiative. It is spontaneous, dynamic, interactive, and dialogical.

Bruner and Sherwood describe how, over time, the child takes a more and more active part in the game. Gradually, actions and initiatives carried out by the mother are taken over by the child. It is exactly when the child shows signs of being able to take over some piece of the action, that the mother scaffolds this takeover, handing over that particular action and guiding the child toward accomplishing it. As noted by the researchers, by 15 months of age, children may invent and control variations on the game, including those where they themselves hide and then reappear with a "Boo!"

For such development to be possible, control must be shared. It is very important that the mother not take initiative away from the baby. Tellingly, the game failed for one mother-child pair when the infant was having trouble hiding his face behind a cloth and the mother took the cloth away to do the masking for him. In response, the infant crawled off, ending the game (1976, p. 282). To be successful, scaffolding requires enticing the child to take as much initiative as possible.

Scaffolding in a Tutoring Setting

What understandings about scaffolding in Bruner's peekaboo study were obscured in a subsequent study of tutoring interactions? What have been the ramifications for common interpretations of the opportunities to scaffold learning?

The study that introduced scaffolding into an education context (specifically, in relation to one-on-one tutoring) was conducted after the peekaboo study, although published the same year (Wood, Bruner, and Ross, 1976). As we will see, the authors summarized the findings of their study in a way that did not highlight the two main ideas from the peekaboo study: (1) the real power of scaffolding lies not in the setup or structure of a task (i.e., the syntax of the peekaboo game), however important that may be, but in the non-rule-bound parts of the task, that is, the moments of agency when the child introduces something new and, perhaps, unexpected; and (2) a learner's agency is promoted by gradual handover of the task to the learner.

This study was based on one-time, one-on-one tutoring sessions with 33 preschool children who were tutored to construct shapes using specially designed wooden blocks. The tutor's role was to assist the children based on their activity patterns — their trials, attempts, and failures, for example. The behaviors of the tutor and the children were scored according to a set of criteria aimed at establishing the amount, patterns, and effects of assistance.

Funded by the U.S. National Institutes of Health during a period of intense interest in programmed learning, the study had as a particular goal "to examine a 'natural' tutorial in the hope of gaining knowledge about natural as well as automated teaching tasks" (Wood et al., p. 89). The authors appear to have summarized their findings accordingly, with a focus on the *task*, that is, the components of the task as it was carried out, rather than on the scaffolding that took place during the task. Given that there was only a single tutoring session per learner, data about handover/takeover was limited in any case. Thus, it was the task itself that the study emphasized and on which subsequent researchers and educators focused.

Wood and colleagues summarized the findings of their tutoring study in terms of six "essential elements" of scaffolding:

1. Recruiting interest in the task,

2. Reduction in degrees of freedom (simplifying the task),

3. Maintaining pursuit of the goal,

4. Marking critical features of discrepancies between what has been produced and the ideal solution,

5. Controlling frustration and risk during problem solving, and

6. Demonstrating an idealized version of the act to be produced. (p. 98)

This list has entered the education literature and teacher guides as representing the defining features of scaffolding. As teachers, we can relate to those six elements, with some caveats about point 2.[1] They are common-sense considerations that good teachers bear in mind when they design and carry out lessons and activities. However, the focus of this list is on the role of the tutor (or teacher); left out is the learner's active involvement, the learner's agency.

Yet when we read the study carefully, we come across some descriptions of the tutoring procedures that do remind us of the central features from the peekaboo study:

---

1 See the discussion on pages 46–48 of the important difference between simplifying the task and amplifying the access.

- The tutor's aim with every child was "to allow him to do as much as possible for himself...the child's success or failure at any point in time thus determined the tutor's next level of instruction" (p. 90).

- The children were divided into groups of three-, four-, and five-year-olds, and the researchers looked at how the tutoring varied from one group to the other. It turned out that with the three-year-olds the predominant intervention was "showing," with the four-year-olds it was "telling," and with the five-year-olds it was "confirming and checking constructions." In other words, the kind of intervention differed depending on the level of skill the children demonstrated (p. 96).

Although these two features did not make it to the final list of six shown above, they are, according to the peekaboo study, the essential elements in the *process* of scaffolding. Restated briefly, they refer to the increasing agency and autonomy of the child and to the handover-takeover process. By combining the six elements highlighted in the tutoring study with the two elements that define scaffolding in the peekaboo study, we can hold on to a more generative notion of scaffolding as we look at its application in classrooms, stressing the idea that scaffolding entails support that, by being "just right," allows the creation of novel performances, or actions that promise new learning.

Scaffolding in Classrooms

How do we apply the structures and processes of scaffolding in the classroom without losing track of the original power of Bruner's insights?

In classrooms, as in peekaboo games and tutoring interactions, the structures and the processes of scaffolding both have a role. Like the rules, or syntax, of peekaboo, well-designed lessons and learning tasks allow for instances in which learner agency, scaffolded by a range of dialogic interactions, results in learning and development.

Learning Tasks That Promote Autonomy

How does the structure of classroom learning tasks allow for scaffolding to occur?

If the combination of the obligatory and optional rules that Bruner first described in the structure of the peekaboo game is applied in teaching, classroom tasks have (more or less) predictable structures and are carried out by way of (more or less) unpredictable processes. For example, the teacher may introduce a jigsaw reading activity that is carefully structured but contains group discussions, consensus building, and short group presentations. During these discussions and presentations, students may come up with novel and unexpected ideas that enliven the lesson and open up new opportunities for teaching and learning (see examples of such tasks in chapter 6).

The structure (the way the task or game is set up, with its predictable rules and recurring ritual elements) *only* exists to enable the unexpected, the unpredictable to occur. The framework of the task makes the innovation possible.

This interdependence of the *rules* and *how the game is played* (in other words, of *structure* and *process*) is an extremely important observation for application of scaffolding in classrooms. Scaffolding is not simply the setting up of task structures to "help" the learner or the design of activities to make learner participation easier. More importantly, it is a dynamic and contingent reaction to something new that the learner introduces into any classroom work. When this unexpected innovation (initiated by the learner) appears, *then and only then* does the teacher's real scaffolding work begin.

The essence of scaffolding is not something planned into the design of a lesson or syllabus. It is, by definition, unplanned, something that happens on the spot when a learner says or does something that foreshadows a new development or a promising direction. This does not mean, of course, that the planned design is useless. Indeed, it is the expert (but flexible and adaptable) design that makes possible a student's innovative actions and budding developments. In addition, the learner's initiatives, while unpredictable to a certain degree, are instigated, invited, and promoted by features of task design and the teacher's proleptic[2] interactions with the class.

The metaphor of the scaffold works in this way: the builders put a scaffold around a building that needs to be renovated, but the scaffold itself is only useful to the extent that it facilitates the work that is to be done. The scaffold is constantly changed, dismantled, extended, and adapted in accordance with the needs of the workers. In itself, it has no value.

This idea, that quality education is (or should be) all about capitalizing on departures from the well-trodden path, is nothing new. As expressed by the influential curriculum reformer Lawrence Stenhouse,

---

2 Prolepsis refers to foreshadowing the future in the present. The teacher acts as if learners have abilities that, in fact, they do not yet have. This, according to Vygotsky, is an essential condition for the development of those abilities (Bakhurst, 1991, p. 67).

Education as induction into knowledge is successful to the extent that it makes the behavioral outcomes of the students unpredictable. (1975, pp. 82–3)

In our own thinking, we take this one step further. Rather than simply accepting that unpredictable outcomes are desirable in the long run, we focus on the unpredictable as a key feature of pedagogy in the here and now. Our emphasis is on how to handle the unpredictable, as introduced by students' thinking, acting, and communicating behaviors.

From this perspective, the work of scaffolding learning may *begin* with tasks that allow for learner agency and initiative — in other words, tasks that support learner autonomy (Deci and Flaste, 1995). Such tasks are structured carefully, neither to lead to chaos nor to stifle the learners' development. The structures are not rigid, but they are supportive and robust. Once again, we are reminded of the delicate balance between structure and process, but we draw the conclusion that *the purpose of the structure is to facilitate the process*. That process goes back to the particular kinds of interactions that are needed to promote autonomy.

Teacher Interactions That Promote Autonomy

Why might so many teacher-student interactions fail to support student agency?

When we looked at the essence of scaffolding in the peekaboo study, we found that it is driven by some innovation or emergent understanding or skill demonstrated by the child when that child, in a way, gets ahead of herself. The mother notices this emergent behavior and helps the child to develop it. In this way, scaffolding is contingent on some self-initiated action by the child: it is based on the child's agency. The principle is no different in the classroom. For the scaffolding process to work, the teacher's role is not to control the learner but to support and encourage the learner's emergent autonomy.

In the past, scaffolding sometimes has been associated with the IRF (Initiation-Response-Feedback or Follow-up) or IRE (Initiation-Response-Evaluation) questioning pattern in teacher-student dialogue. But consider the parallel teacher-student IRE/IRF interactions in figure 2. As simple examples of English-language practice (in this case, giving travel directions), neither dialogue could be called an instance of scaffolding, even though in the dialogue on the left the teacher offers evaluative "assistance" to the learner. In the dialogue on the left, the student has no initiative or autonomy and no control over what is being said, by whom, or when. She is merely designated to answer the question and must rely on the teacher's approval to know if she completed the task satisfactorily. The interaction, including even the student's contributions, "belongs" to the teacher, who controls the agenda. It is difficult to see any meaningful handover/take-over possibilities. In the dialogue on the right, however, instead of "assisting" the learner, at the end of the practice, the teacher's simple "Thanks!" injects a small nod to the student's agency. The teacher has apparently made a decision that the student's effort should be validated rather than evaluated and improved.

Two additional dialogues, below and on page 27, demonstrate the clear difference between an instance of IRE and an instance of scaffolded teacher-student dialogue that promotes student autonomy. In the first, Pauline Gibbons (2002) provides a crisp example of IRE.

> Teacher: What season comes after fall?
> Student: Winter.
> Teacher: Good girl.

Figure 2. Teacher Decision Making in a Practice Dialogue: No Scaffolding

Form-Oriented IRE		Meaning-Oriented IRF	
Teacher:	Excuse me.	Teacher:	Excuse me.
Student:	Yes?	Student:	Yes?
Teacher:	Can you tell me how I can get to Highway 1 from here?	Teacher:	Can you tell me how I can get to Highway 1 from here?
Student:	No problem! You go straight that way and see traffic light. When traffic light, you …left, then go, eh, go more …straight and then the Highway 1, you will see it.	Student:	No problem! You go straight that way and see traffic light. When traffic light, you …left, then go, eh, go more …straight and then the Highway 1, you will see it.
Teacher:	Okay. Listen. Go straight TO the traffic light, turn left, and go straight ahead UNTIL you see the sign for Highway 1.	Teacher:	Thanks!
Student:	Ehm…go straight TO traffic light…(etc.)	Student:	You welcome!

In this first exchange, the teacher knows the answer and is checking to see whether the student does. When the student answers, the teacher evaluates and approves the student's answer. Notice the differences in the classroom dialogue below:

Student:	It's like everybody should get the same rights and protection, no matter like race, religion.
Teacher:	Yeah. Everybody.
Student:	No matter if they are a citizen or illegal, they should get the same protection.
Teacher:	I agree with you, but why do you say that with confidence?
Student:	Because it says that.
Teacher:	Because it says that?

Student:	Also because it [the 14th Amendment] says it should not deny any person of the right to life, liberty, and property without due process.
Teacher:	Okay, not any *citizen?*
Student:	Any *person.*
Teacher:	Okay, so is the 14th Amendment helpful to you?

Student: Also because it [the 14th Amendment] says it should not deny any person of the right to life, liberty, and property without due process.

Teacher: Okay, not any *citizen?*

Student: Any *person.*

Teacher: Okay, so is the 14th Amendment helpful to you?

(Price and Walqui, 2001)

In this second interaction, the teacher promotes the learner's autonomy, first by prompting her to justify or elaborate her thinking and then by connecting the student's learning to her experience as an immigrant. By encouraging the student to speak for herself, to be precise, and to present a clear argument, the teacher scaffolds the student's disciplinary knowledge and language learning simultaneously.

Interactions Beyond "Expert-Novice" That Scaffold Learning

What evidence might you cite for a ZPD in which scaffolding possibilities arise from interaction with equal peers, less capable peers, and oneself, in addition to adults or more capable peers?

It is not surprising that for many people the "expert-novice" relationship characterizes both scaffolding and the ZPD. The original contexts of scaffolding were mother-infant interaction and tutor-child problem solving, and the most often quoted definitions of the ZPD refer to guidance from an adult or a more competent peer (see chapter 1). In addition, it is commonly believed that, for learning to occur, knowledge or a skill must be transmitted *from* a more knowledgeable person *to* a less knowledgeable one. After all, it seems reasonable to think, "I can only learn from someone who knows more than I do." This assumption is by no means limited to scaffolding and the ZPD. As an example, a strong trend in Second Language Acquisition (SLA) theory assumes that the most profitable interaction is that between a native speaker (or at least a more proficient nonnative speaker) and a learner (e.g., Long, 1996).

On the other hand, many accounts of learning do not follow this intuitively plausible pattern. In the work of several researchers (Donato, 1994; Gibbons, 2002; Mercer, 1995; Rogoff, 1995), the idea of scaffolding has been expanded to include a relationship of equal knowledge — a group of equally knowledgeable learners working on a shared task, for example. In such circumstances, students create zones of proximal development for each other and engage in mutual scaffolding (again illustrating Vygotsky's remarks about the child being "a head taller than himself" in play).

In one such instance, Richard Donato (1994) conducted a microanalysis of the interactions among students working in groups on picture-completion puzzles. He was able to document the process by which the students gained new knowledge even when *none* of them had that knowledge in the first place. Donato's research is an example that supports Urie Bronfenbrenner's (1979) social ecological theory of human development: ideas emerge in interaction, are shared with peers, and are further developed in the interaction.

To informally illustrate this principle of collaborative scaffolding to his graduate students, author van Lier designed an outrageously difficult grammar test. On several occasions, he passed it out and asked the students to look it over and say whether they thought they could complete it by themselves. The students would complain that the test was impossible. He would then guarantee that, even though the test was impossible for each individual student, they would be able to solve all items if they worked together as a class. The instructor just stepped back and let them have at it, monitoring the spirited debates around the room, sometimes just pointing with a finger to another student "over there" when one student "over here" seemed to be stuck — in a sense, directing the "traffic" around the room.

Invariably, the whole test was completed successfully before the end of class. This collaborative construction was more than just putting together bits of knowledge that each student has. Instead, students found that one half-idea invites completion, one thought leads to another, and one tentative step opens up a direction to explore. Students came away with a profound respect for the power of collaborative problem solving.

In addition to expert-novice interaction and interaction between equal peers, van Lier (1996, 2004) has proposed two other contexts in which students can work within their ZPDs (as shown in figure 3): a learner teaching

Figure 3. ZPD: Expanding the Construct

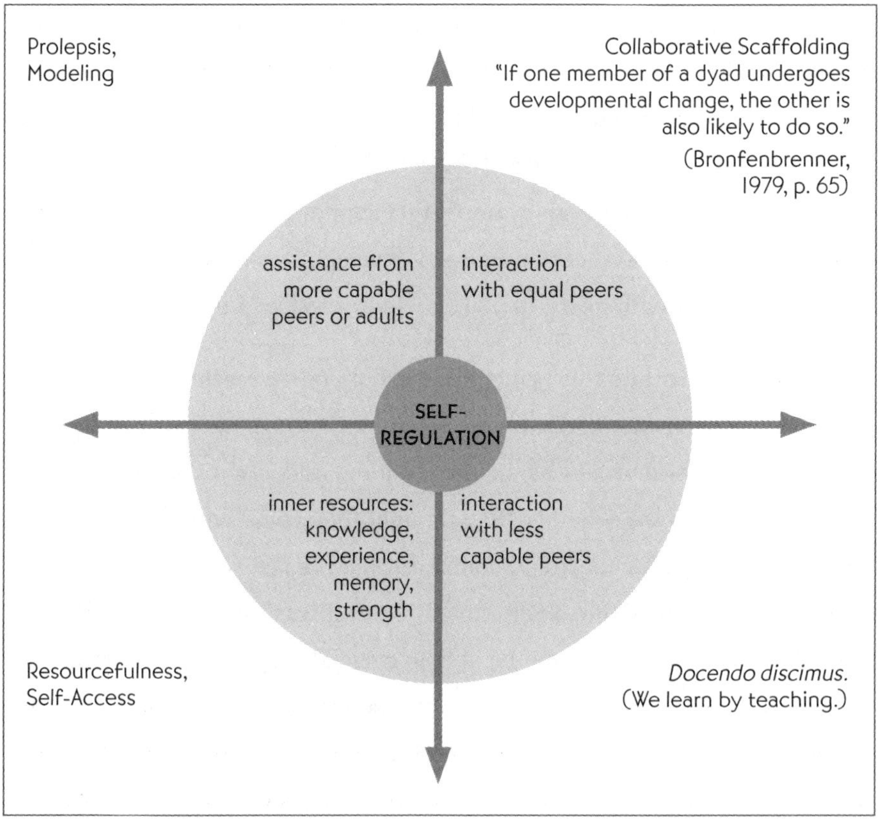

(Based on van Lier, 2004, p. 158)

another learner (i.e., interaction between a novice and a less capable peer), and a learner working alone. When students work with someone who has less understanding, they can benefit from the opportunity to verbalize, clarify, and extend their own knowledge of the subject matter. Working alone, students can benefit by using internalized teaching and learning strategies, inner speech, resources in their environment, and experimentation.

The following extract from a lesson on Robert Frost's poem "The Road Not Taken" (see chapter 1 for another extract from this lesson) demonstrates van Lier's expansion of the ZPD construct to include scaffolding when a student learns by working with a less capable peer and, also, when the same student calls on her own inner resources, her resourcefulness.

In the lesson, students must collaborate to construct a phrase that explains the state of mind described by the poet. The two girls working together are an interesting pair because although Student 3 is the more capable, Student 2 drives their collaboration and creates the opportunity for Student 3 to sort out her own thinking by explaining to Student 2 the essence of the poem:

Student 2: It's supposed to be like a decision...We should write a little bit like a hard word, you know?...How about this, "And then looked down far as I could"?...How about this, how about, "I looked far for the right decision"? No, it has to rhyme!

The condition that the phrase must rhyme is self-imposed by Student 2 but accepted by Student 3. Student 2 continues, still trying to get them started.

Student 2: How about this, "I'm Robert Frost, I've got to decide which path to take, right or wrong." No, "right or wrong" ruined it. *(begins writing)* "I'm Robert Frost, I have to choose, but it's difficult for me, Robert Frost, to find the truth."

Student 3: I don't know...write it, write it. Write all of it, then we can fix it.

Student 2: "I'm Robert Frost, I have a path to choose. It's hard for me" —

Student 3: "Robert Frost"—

Student 2: "to find the truth." It's like a rap.

Student 3: Let me see *(reading what Student 2 has written)*, "I'm Robert Frost, I have a path to choose"—

Student 2: "it's hard for me to find the truth." Like "truth" and "Frost" kind of go together...

Student 3: "I'm Robert Frost, I have a path to choose"—

Student 2: *(With sudden excitement)* Oh! Oh! "to choose the good or to choose the wrong."

Student 3: *(Matter-of-factly)* Uh, "to choose the right or to choose the wrong."

Student 2: Yeah, yeah, "to choose the right or to choose the wrong."

Student 3's first move was to improve on Student 2's language use, and now she addresses Student 2's idea.

Student 3: But he doesn't know which one is wrong...

Student 2: Okay, "I'm Robert Frost, I have a path to choose *(writing the new ending)*, it's up to me to find the truth."

Student 3: Better. I think this one makes more sense and it explains more.

Student 2: Yeah, but he still needs to choose, "to choose the right or to choose the wrong."

Student 3: Wait.

Student 2: No, no, now it doesn't make sense, "to choose the right or to choose the wrong."

Student 3: It doesn't make sense because he doesn't know which one is right, which one is wrong. That's the point of asking himself which way to go.

Student 2 accepts the explanation offered by Student 3 and restarts the construction process.

Student 2: Okay, "I'm Robert Frost, I have a path to choose. I might choose the right, but I might be...?

Student 3: *(Pointing)* This is good until this part. We have to think up of the ending.

Student 2: "I might choose the right, but I might be..." Only "wrong" goes there.

Recognizing that they face a problem finding something that rhymes with "right," Student 3 uses her own resourcefulness, deciding to locate a source of potential information.

Student 3: Where's the dictionary?

(Cohen and Walqui, 2007)

To summarize, we have seen examples of ways learners use resources in all four quadrants in the expanded construct of the ZPD — from Bruner's peekaboo study where learning is scaffolded by someone more capable, to van Lier's linguistics classrooms where peers create knowledge that none had individually, to Student 3 deepening her own understanding by teaching a less capable peer, and to Student 3's demonstration of resourcefulness in the simple act of going to the dictionary.

In each of the four different participation contexts for task-based interaction, the scaffolding that occurs incorporates some or all of the six features described below.

Features of Pedagogical Scaffolding

How do the features of pedagogical scaffolding apply especially to English language learners?

The features of pedagogical scaffolding represent a consolidation of points made earlier in this chapter: learner agency, as described in the peekaboo study; scaffolding, as summarized in the tutoring study; and the idea that scaffolding applies beyond the teacher-learner, or expert-novice, context. The features outlined here reflect that learning can — and does — happen in all sorts of ways, some predictable, many not. Figure 4 (page 34) outlines the features of pedagogical scaffolding in a sequence that flows from planned to improvised, from "designed-in" to

Figure 4. Features of Pedagogical Scaffolding

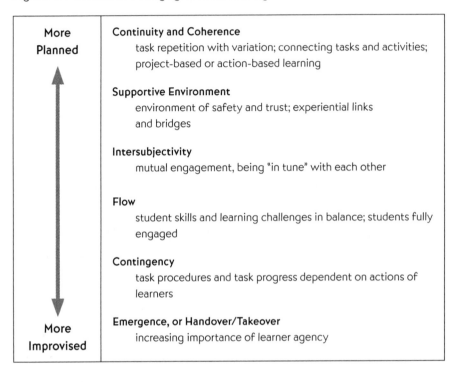

More Planned	Continuity and Coherence task repetition with variation; connecting tasks and activities; project-based or action-based learning
↑	Supportive Environment environment of safety and trust; experiential links and bridges
	Intersubjectivity mutual engagement, being "in tune" with each other
	Flow student skills and learning challenges in balance; students fully engaged
↓	Contingency task procedures and task progress dependent on actions of learners
More Improvised	Emergence, or Handover/Takeover increasing importance of learner agency

"interactional" (Gibbons, 2005), from the macro level of a syllabus or curriculum to the micro level of moment-to-moment interaction. The arrow on the left of the diagram suggests that the features move from more-planned and larger scale at the top to more-improvised and smaller scale at the bottom as the structure and process flow together. In the discussion of each feature, we have an opportunity to consider how these apply in particular to our work with English learners.

In teaching, the feature of *continuity and coherence* derives from the understanding that a classroom is, in a sense, a culture of its own. As such, it has rituals that characterize it and keep it together, some that stay constant and others that vary and evolve. In addition, classrooms have tasks and activities that occur again and again, but with variation and room for improvisation. Within these recurring, stable aspects of the classroom, learners find stability, as well as opportunities to innovate and take initiative.

As described in chapters 4, 5, and 6, much of the QTEL curriculum is built around a set of organizing structures (e.g., the three-part lesson plan and steps in teaching a genre) and repeated tasks and variations on those tasks, such as jigsaw reading, round robin, and collaborative posters. When a lesson has a certain familiarity, English language learners can focus on features of language, rather than having their attention diverted by unfamiliar lesson procedures or tasks. Instead of sorting out lesson directions, they can practice listening and speaking in a meaningful context. Having *continuity and coherence* in their curriculum and instruction provides English language learners with a steady platform from which to venture out in new linguistic directions.

The feature of a *supportive environment* derives from the understanding that if learners want to try something new, to be creative, to explore the outer edges of their knowledge and skill base (in their ZPD), they must feel safe and trusted and must know that any mistakes or failures will not be held against them. This kind of contextual support also means that the environment promotes access to the means and goals of exploration. For example, task directions and formulaic expressions for participating in task-related conversations (e.g., I agree with...because; A different idea is...; I am not sure, but it seems to me...) are posted on classroom walls.

For English learners, having a *supportive environment* means they can trust the teacher and their fellow learners to be supportive and tolerant of their attempts to try something new, even if they might not be fully successful yet. Just as *continuity and coherence* create a cognitive and conceptual safety platform, so a *supportive environment* creates a social and interpersonal safety platform.

Mutual engagement, or *intersubjectivity,* implies that the larger-scale features of scaffolding are in place. The *structure* of a coherent and supportive environment enables the *process* of intersubjectivity. Feeling safe, trusted, and "in tune," students engage in collaborative action that makes them want to work together toward a common goal.

For English learners, *intersubjectivity* means they listen attentively to what others have to say, and at the same time, others listen to them constructively and with interest. They are happy to help others without being pushy and are comfortable asking for help without feeling embarrassed. They are willing to invest time and energy in understanding each other, knowing full well that their expressions may still be imprecise and that their accents may sometimes obscure their meanings.

When learners are working on tasks and projects that engage them and that have support structures and room for autonomy, when skills and challenges are in perfect balance, they may experience a state of *flow* (Csikszentmihalyi, 1990). In these instances, learners are engaged in the activity for the sake of the activity itself and are absorbed in their work. They may not even hear the bell or the teacher's voice saying that it's time to pack up.

As with any learners, when English language learners experience *flow,* they are working on challenging, meaningful, and relevant activities, and they are doing so not simply because they are told to or for a grade, but because the activities are intrinsically motivating.

Scaffolding is *contingent* on the learners' agency. Task procedures and task progress depend on initiatives taken by learners in the context of interaction with their peers, their teacher, or internally. One action or utterance calls forth the next one, and each action or utterance relates back to previous ones, just as in a focused conversation where every turn points back to the previous one and looks forward to the next one.

For English learners, *contingency* means there are clear reasons and goals for an activity: there is a reason for engaging in it, and every step naturally feeds into the next step. The language used is supported by what has been said so far, and it contributes to what is said next.

Finally, the feature of *emergence,* or *handover/takeover,* may be the most crucial of all. Teacher (or peer) support is gradually removed (it "fades," as some researchers say) in line with the learner's growing, or emerging, competence. As increasing pieces of the action are handed over to the learner, the learner herself also has the opportunity to take over when she feels this is possible or desirable. The interplay between handover and takeover delicately nurtures the learner's development.

For English learners, *emergence,* or *handover/takeover,* means they become increasingly autonomous. They find their own voice and take initiative in proposing, planning, constructing, and reflecting on subject area tasks. In this way, they build their English language identity and appropriate the language along with it.

Together, the features of pedagogical scaffolding described above serve as guidelines for constructing a learning environment that is both controlled and free or, we might say, that moves between control (structure) and freedom (process), between constraining and releasing (Valsiner, 2006), letting go and pulling back, giving free rein and reining in. The structures that *allow for* scaffolding are integrated with the processes that *are* scaffolding. The continuum that begins with the structural feature of continuity and coherence moves to the procedural feature of handover/takeover.

Before concluding this discussion of scaffolding, we would like to high-light one approach that applies in all instances of scaffolding the academic development of English language learners, that is, the practice of *amplifying* access to language and learning, in contrast to *simplifying* language and tasks (Walqui, 1992).

Amplify, Don't Simplify!

In what ways could you call amplification the antidote to simplification?

Earlier in the chapter, in discussing the tutoring study, we hung a caution flag on the phrase "simplifying the task," as used by Wood et al. (1976) in referring to an element of scaffolding: "Reduction in degrees of freedom, or simplifying the task."

"Degrees of freedom" is a technical term, often used in statistical measure-ment, that refers to the amount of variation in a task or process. If a learner has a complex task to accomplish and if, at any point in time, there are multiple possible ways to proceed with the task, the learner might feel over-whelmed. In such a case, the tutor might hint, or prompt the learner, as to the best next step. This is an example of reducing the degrees of freedom. But is it also an example of "simplifying the task?" Not if the goal — the knowledge or skill to be attained — remains the same, with the task simply broken down into more manageable subactivities so that the learner's prog-ress is scaffolded by judicious guidance only as needed.

The word "simplify" is a dangerous one. It reminds us of "dumbed-down" lessons, simplified language use, and reduced expectations and goals. As we have seen, this is clearly not what Wood et al. had in mind, but their particular choice of language remains potentially misleading. Numerous educators have insisted strongly that simplifying the task (in the sense of reducing the objectives or choosing easier tasks) is not part of scaffolding.

In the professional development institutes that QTEL offers, the advice "Amplify, don't simplify!" is often voiced. Researchers Clay and Cazden refer to "increasing accessibility" rather than "simplifying the task" (1992, p. 120). Similarly, Tharp and Gallimore see scaffolding as simplifying the learner's role, not the task:

> Scaffolding...does not involve simplifying the task; it holds the task difficulty constant, while simplifying the child's role by means of graduated assistance from the adult/expert. (1988, p. 33)

This remark is well within the spirit of Wood et al.'s use of "simplify." However, even here we might worry that this simplification is based on the judgment of the tutor/teacher; what is to ensure that this is not a *mis*judgment? In other words, what is to prevent the teacher from thinking or feeling, "Oh, they cannot do that" or "My students are not that smart," and so give the students watered-down texts and easy tasks? In fact, in accordance with the idea of scaffolding, it may well be that students under-perform because their teachers under-expect or misinterpret: the mother takes the peekaboo cloth away; the game fails.

A classroom example of such derailment of the scaffolding process is when a teacher immediately corrects every error a learner makes by providing the correct word or phrase. This practice may have two (or more) undesirable consequences. First, it interrupts the learner's expression of the ideas she or he was formulating; second, it does not leave room for possible self-correction, awareness raising, or other processes that involve the learner's agency. In addition, of course, it may demotivate or distress the learner, and it may make the learner more dependent on the teacher (thus negating the main scaffolding principle of *agency*).

When teaching English learners, amplifying students' access to the linguistic and extralinguistic context means providing students with more than a single opportunity to come to terms with the language and concepts involved. Multiple clues and perspectives increase students' opportunities to construct understanding. As Gibbons (2003) puts it, the teacher provides "message abundancy."[3] In the following extract from Tony DeFazio's high school classroom for English language learners, we see that after students have read the assignment directions, the teacher amplifies their access to the instructions — and to academic language that is by no means simplified:

> You can use your native language to write your letters, but if you do this, there is a caveat...a stipulation...there is something you have to do. You need to summarize your ideas in a paragraph in English.
>
> (DeFazio and Walqui, 2001)

In addition to the literal abundancy of the teacher's oral message, he punctuates it with verbal emphasis and body language as he elaborates. Students cannot fail to understand the assignment or the teacher's high expectations for their learning and engagement.

Conclusion

In this chapter, we have reframed an understanding of "scaffolding" from its origins in studies of adult-child interactions in peekaboo games and tutoring, emphasizing the role of learner agency and contingent responses. At the same time that we have clarified scaffolding as a process that can happen only in the learner's zone of proximal development, we have also described structures that promote learner agency and thus allow for scaffolding to occur. This structure-process tension means that pedagogical scaffolding can be described as having features that range from planned to

---

3   In linguistics, this concept is sometimes referred to as "redundancy," but the term *abundancy* avoids the connotation that, somehow, the extra information might be superfluous.

improvised — from the macro level of a coherent curriculum to the meso level of well-structured tasks to the micro level of in-the-moment handover and takeover as scaffolding gradually fades.

We have seen that the process of scaffolding is not limited to expert-novice interactions. Instances in which the learner interacts with equal peers, interacts with less capable peers, or operates alone can also be structured to allow for learning to be scaffolded. For English language learners in particular, all of these instances benefit from, and likely require, message abundancy — amplification, not simplification.

In the next chapter, we take a look at the *language* of messages and what we know about language learning, especially academic language learning.

CHAPTER 3

THE ROLE
OF LANGUAGE
AND LANGUAGE
LEARNING

All teachers who have English language learners in their classroom are language teachers, regardless of their main job to teach language arts, social studies, math, or science. In addition to teaching their subject matter, these teachers need to provide challenging, well supported, and effective disciplinary language instruction. However, for teachers who use a content-based approach or teach mainstream subjects, integrating a focus on language is one of the hardest things to do. These skills do not come automatically with the job of being a subject matter teacher or even an ESL teacher. They require sustained thinking, reflection, and development; the issues involved are complex and multifaceted. In this chapter, we consider the difficulties and possibilities of focusing on language within a subject matter classroom.

Language Development

Why do students who are otherwise fluent in English often struggle with subject matter language?

Well over two decades ago, Jim Cummins (1984) drew attention to problems with how instruction for immigrant students was determined. These students were routinely tested for their English language proficiency by means of quick tests of oral comprehension and the production of everyday conversational language. If they seemed to do all right on these tests, they were placed in regular classrooms and deemed to be ready for mainstream instruction. When these students subsequently struggled in their subject matter classes, their failure was blamed on lack of academic abilities, motivation, or home support, and they were often placed in special education classes. Not surprisingly, dropout rates were very high among these students.

Arguably, the situation is not all that different now. Learners, teachers, and policymakers alike generally seem to think that "knowing English" is "knowing English," regardless of the situation in which the language is used. The huge gap between conversational English and the requirements of academic language use is not often appreciated. It's all just English, right?

Yet, a bit of reflection will show that, even as native speakers, we are not always equally skilled in using our own language in different contexts and for different purposes. We may be quite comfortable cracking jokes and telling stories around the dinner table, explaining why candidate X is preferable to candidate Y, and so on; but we might be less comfortable describing to a doctor why we don't feel well or to a car mechanic what exactly those noises are that come out of the engine when we start the car on a cold morning. Alternatively, we might be able to write beautiful poems, yet be unable to participate in small talk at a reception.

Likewise, students who are English language learners have different levels of general abilities and different kinds of interests and skills, all of which are reflected in complex ways in their use of English. These students are not products of one single cookie cutter, and their scores on standardized tests do not tell us who they are and what they might be capable of knowing or doing.

In the sections below, we will examine the differences between conversational language and its more challenging partner — academic language — and, in particular, look at the important notion of *genre*.

Conversational Language

Linguists often claim that by the age of five or so, children have basically mastered the syntax of their native language (Chomsky, 1986; Pinker, 1994). Indeed, children around that age sometimes come up with remarkably complex, grammatically correct utterances. They can also be quite inventive in applying patterns of use that sound plausible, yet do not happen to be part of the language. A child who has climbed into a tree might say, "Can you lower me down?" She might also ask, if she wants to reach the cookies on the top shelf in the kitchen, "Can you higher me up?" In a class of high school English learners, an enthusiastic teacher explaining the word *apathetic* pointed out that the prefix *a-* often means the absence of something, in this case, "without energy" or "without emotion." To elaborate, the teacher gave the paired examples of *political — apolitical, moral — amoral.* In response, one smart student joked, "Teacher, so you are *pathetic?"*

Acknowledging that children and English language learners are capable of coming up with gems of language, there also are many constructions that we would not expect of them. For example, the following extract from a text many students encounter, Richard Wright's *Black Boy,* while easily comprehended, would not likely be part of most adolescents' linguistic repertoire, regardless of their status as native English speaker or English language learner:

> I flayed with tears in my eyes, teeth clenched, stark fear making me throw every ounce of my strength behind each blow. I hit again and again, dropping the money and the grocery list. The boys scattered, yelling, nursing their heads, staring at me in utter disbelief. (p. 18)

The differences between everyday conversational language use and literate, academic (or otherwise specialized) uses of language are often associated with whether the language is used in speech or writing, though things are not quite as simple as that (see, for example, the section on genre below). Jim Cummins (1984) initially proposed a distinction between what he labeled Basic Interpersonal Communication Skills (BICS) and Cognitive Academic Language Proficiency (CALP). That formulation has often been criticized as too simplistic and dichotomous, and Cummins has since elaborated it into a model that distinguishes between the degree of cognitive complexity and the amount of contextual information available (e.g., 1996, p. 57).

Australian researcher Pauline Gibbons identifies such differences in terms of "playground language" and "classroom language":

> This playground language includes the language which enables children to make friends, join in games and take part in a variety of day-to-day activities that develop and maintain social contacts. It usually occurs in face-to-face contact, and is thus highly dependent on the physical and visual context, and on gesture and body language. Fluency with this kind of language is an important part of language development; without it a child is isolated from the normal social life of the playground.

> But playground language is very different from the language that teachers use in the classroom, and from the language that we expect children to learn to use. The language of the playground is not the language associated with learning in mathematics, or social studies, or science. The playground situation does not normally offer children the

opportunity to use such language as: *if we increase the angle by 5 degrees, we could cut the circumference into equal parts.* Nor does it normally require the language associated with the higher order thinking skills, such as hypothesizing, evaluating, inferring, generalizing, predicting or classifying. Yet these are the language functions that are related to learning and the development of cognition; they occur in all areas of the curriculum, and without them a child's potential in academic areas cannot be realized.

(Gibbons, 1991, p. 3, as cited in Cummins, 1996, pp. 56–57)

English language learners may be able to carry on conversations with ease and, perhaps, sound remarkably fluent and native-like. Yet, when it comes to using academic language in reading or writing tasks, they may experience tremendous problems.

Academic Language

As illustrated in the following teacher-student interaction in a class studying brain function (see, also, chapter 5), English language learners who feel comfortable with conversational English may protest against having to practice complex terminology:

> Student 2: But I know English.
>
> Teacher: Yes, but *psychological* English.

This brief exchange between an English language learner and the teacher (Crescenzi and Walqui, 2008) encapsulates the challenge that academic language raises for teachers, as well as for many students (not only English language learners). Teachers of English language learners — and the learners — often find that they need to focus on the language itself in order to get something right, whether in formulating a question, finding a word for an object, writing a description, or any other of the multitude of ways in which language is used in lessons. For example, in the lesson on brain function, students must navigate complex academic terminology, including unfamiliar psychological terms (e.g., *amygdala, frontal lobe, parietal lobe*). Later, when describing a brain injury, they must learn to say things like "penetrated his skull," when they might prefer to say, "went through his head." The following classroom interchange is an example of such linguistic negotiation.

Student 12: *(Reading a proposed answer to group members)* "A tamping rod may have penetrated Phineas Gage's skull."

Student 13: Did you all put that he got that little thing through his head, right?

Student 12: Yeah.

Student 13: Awesome.

Student 4: The rod. The rod may have penetrated

Student 13: Do you have to use a big word like that? I'm just gonna put "went through."

Student 2: *(Teasing)* Oh, put "p" then a dot.

(Crescenzi and Walqui, 2008)

The students in this group encounter the differences between everyday language and academically precise expression. Student 13 resists the "big word" *penetrated,* proposing that "went through" would do just as well. Student 2, in a slightly sarcastic tone, advises Student 13 to compromise, and just write "p." Even English language learners who are quite proficient in everyday language can find that the unfamiliar universe of academic language makes achieving subject matter proficiency a long and hard struggle, one they may especially resist if it causes identity conflicts. In the above example, Student 13 appears reluctant to "play the academic game." As teachers, by paying very close attention to students' interactions during group tasks, we can learn much about how to help them become the practiced users of academic language that they need to be.

A lot of academic language is common across different disciplines. For example, the word *penetrate* that some students had difficulty with in the brain injury lesson is used in different subjects (physics, history, literature, and so on). However, even though the word is the same, its meaning and patterns of use may be quite different. In history, spies may penetrate enemy positions; in literature, a particular turn of phrase may be a penetrating insight; and in science, a chemical may penetrate a rock. Students need to understand how meaning may shift for a single word as its context shifts.

Conversational and Academic Language: A Continuum

Because conversation and academic language use can be seen as opposite ends of a continuum, from informal to formal, and from highly contextualized to highly academic, a key question, and one that drives the work of QTEL, is *How can we use the conversational skills of English language learners to help them build the academic skills that they will increasingly need to be successful in school?*

In recent years, researchers such as Pauline Gibbons and Mary Schleppegrell have focused intently on this question. An important insight of their research is that in order to learn academic registers, that is, the "style" of language that is common in academic fields, learners have to talk about the language they are using. Once they become more aware of the language choices they make, which is to say, become more metalinguistic, everyday language can then form a bridge toward the increasingly complex academic language they need to master. The teacher, through carefully designed activities and scaffolding, leads the students step by step toward using more complex vocabulary and expressions. As in the extract from the brain injury discussion on the preceding page, the student locution "he got that little thing through his head" becomes "a tamping rod penetrated his skull." Later in that same class, when a student describes a brain-injured person who "hears stuff," the teacher takes the time to bring the class around to the description of someone who "has auditory hallucinations" (see the dialogue extract on page 65).

In the classroom, both teacher and learners will switch back and forth between everyday language and academic language as they discuss tasks in a given discipline. However, the teacher nudges the students toward familiarity with academic ways of discussing, reading, and writing. Gradually, the amount of academic language increases, with conversational language beginning to play more of a supporting role.

A good example of the intermingling of conversational and academic language occurs in Tony DeFazio's linguistics class, which we visit frequently in this book. He asks students to write a series of five letters about language to anyone they choose. So students can begin letters with, "Hi, how are you," or even "Hey, what's up," and after some social language begin to tell their addressee about specifics of the linguistics content they are studying. In chapter 6 we cite Stanford professor Kenji Hakuta's comments on one set of these letters, where he notes that the switching between informal and formal style, or "style shifting," shows the sophisticated level of control over language use that these students have developed (see p. 146).

As we point out throughout this book, another way that teachers can help students bridge between informal and more formal language use is by providing formulaic expressions relevant to the academic task at hand. These expressions can be options for responding in a classroom discussion (e.g., "I agree/disagree because…"; "I have a different idea…") or responding in more discipline-specific ways, as when explaining an algebraic equation or making a historical claim. (See, for example, the discussion of supportive environment on page 35 in chapter 2 and the discussion of formulaic expressions and fluency on page 70 later in this chapter.)

In addition to learning such useful phrases, learners need to master such devices as logical connectors (e.g., in other words, however, because) and the commonly used practice in academic texts of *nominalization,* that is, turning a verb or a phrase into a noun, thus making the ideas more abstract and anonymous, and, at the same time, making the text much more dense and compact. Here, from a study by Mary Schleppegrell (forthcoming), is an example of nominalization taken from a grade 11 history textbook:

> The destruction of the buffalo and removal of Native Americans to reservations emptied the land for grazing cattle.

As Schleppegrell suggests, if we were to rewrite this text in more everyday language, it would come out somewhat as follows:

> Settlers and hunters killed all the buffalo and the government forced all the Native Americans to leave their lands and move to reservations. Because the animals and people who had lived on the plains were gone, the land was available, so ranchers began to raise cattle.

Instead of 18 words, the text is now 46 words. As Schleppegrell notes (and see also Gibbons, 2009), the heavily nominalized and condensed text from the history textbook above is extremely hard to process, especially for English language learners. It is an even more complex linguistic and cognitive task for students to *produce* this kind of nominalized academic prose. We can conclude that the mastery of academic language is an enormous challenge for English language learners, one that requires high levels of support.

In addition to guiding students toward academic uses of English by highlighting and talking about the different uses, mixing everyday language with academic expressions, and allowing students to become accustomed to using language in those ways, teachers must prepare students to understand different *genres,* such as letters, scientific reports, stories, poems, descriptions, political debates, and so on, across and within disciplines. We will discuss different genres in the next section.

Genre

Although many academic terms may vary in meaning across subjects, every subject matter area also has its own vocabulary; disciplinary metaphors; ways of explaining things; examples to illustrate its laws, principles, and processes; common approaches to solving its problems; and so on. The language of mathematics is different from that of history, and science uses language differently from language arts. The study of such similarities and differences in language use across and within disciplines is called genre analysis or genre theory. English language learners encounter and need to understand academic language as it is presented in many different genres. Examples referred to in this book include Robert Frost's poem "The Road Not Taken"; Richard Wright's memoir, *Black Boy;* expository writing and nonfiction narrative about brain structure and function; mathematical proofs; and task directions and expository writing about linguistics.

Figure 5 (pages 54–56) shows excerpts from some of these genres in the left column. The differences among these texts are quite appar (pagesent. The poem features rhyme, rhythm, and metaphor. The memoir includes direct speech and dramatic action language. The case study is characterized by descriptive precision. Complex vocabulary is crucial to the geometry text. The directions to students are embedded in a personal letter, which includes reasons for those directions.

In the right column, the examples show a variety of ways in which English language learners work with these texts. Students reading a Robert Frost poem struggle first to understand the literal meaning of two roads diverging in a wood, before they can recognize the metaphor that the poem offers.

In the next example, students have prepared to read from Wright's *Black Boy* by sharing personal anecdotes that in some way anticipate the incident in the text. In the extract included here, after reading the memoir text, a boy from the Dominican Republic spontaneously relates Wright's experience to one of his own.

The teacher introducing brain injury case studies has asked students to share accidents that happened to friends or family members. These stories set the scene for the more formal case descriptions, which students then read and discuss in groups. In the extract that is included, a student reports his group's attempt to summarize their reading in academic language, and the teacher probes for the meaning under the words.

In the lesson on linguistics, the teacher writes a letter to the students, outlining a project in which students are to write five letters about language to a person of their choice. The assignment deliberately blends personal elements with academic explanations and descriptions about language, thus providing a way into the academic discipline of linguistics. In the extract included here, one student reads part of a letter he has drafted during the lesson. We can see his use of academic language ("characteristics to communicate") alongside more informal language ("you know what I'm saying?").

In a mathematics classroom, students have been using academic language to discuss how they solved geometry problems. In the extract, the teacher continues to work with them on understanding the precise mathematical definition of the term *similar*. One student ventures the everyday meaning of "alike in some way," and other students help out with the necessary conditions for geometric figures to be similar.

What these extracts suggest is that by combining academic texts of various genres with engaging and stimulating tasks, teachers can gradually apprentice their English language learners into using academic language in spoken and written form, without, as discussed below, threatening students' identities.

Figure 5. Sample Student Experiences with Different Genres

Text	Student Work
Excerpt from "A Road Not Taken" (Frost, 1916) ...I shall be telling this with a sigh Somewhere ages and ages hence: Two roads diverged in a wood, and I — I took the one less traveled by, And that has made all the difference.	*Partners have been asked to discuss what the poet is trying to say, what he wants the reader to know.* Student 1: If he wouldn't take the road like maybe he wouldn't be like the place that he was. Student 2: In that moment? Student 1: (*Nods*) He would like in a whole different place. Student 2: He would be in a different place? Student 1: (*Nods*) Student 2: If he wouldn't take that way, he would be in another place? He wouldn't be in that place right now? *Several interchanges later, the students are able to articulate the poem's essential metaphor.* Student 1: If he didn't take that one, that would change his life. (Cohen and Walqui, 2007)
Excerpt from *Black Boy* (Wright, 1945) They surrounded me quickly and began to grab for my hand. I'll kill you, I threatened. They closed in. In blind fear I let the stick fly, feeling it crack against a boy's skull. I swung again, lamming another skull, then another.	*A student spontaneously relates the text to his own experience.* Student: This story remind me something that happen to me in my country. Teacher: It happened to you in your country? Student: Yeah. I was playing like in front of my house with my game. I had a lot of toys, because my father always sent me some toys. And I was there, and like two kids, they pass and they see me. They were like thirteen, and I was like ten. And they take my toys. And I was like scared, and I let them take them. I don't do nothing. And when I went inside my house, I say, "Mommy! They take my toys!" And she say, "What? They take what?" And she make me go and get it. When I came back, I came with my nose broke. They broke my nose. (Ng and Walqui, 2005a)

Text	Student Work
Excerpt from Brain Injury Case Study Phineas Gage was foreman of a work gang blasting and blowing up rock to clear the roadbed for a new rail line outside the town of Cavendish, Vermont. To get the job done, workers drilled a hole into a body of rock. Then, it was Gage's duty to fill the hole with explosive gunpowder, add a fuse, cover the gunpowder with sand, and pack the charge down with a long tamping iron before lighting the fuse. On September 13, 1848, possibly because Gage omitted the sand, the tamping rod came into direct contact with the gunpowder, causing an unexpected explosion that drove the rod back out of the hole and through his skull.	*Students report to group members about different case studies of brain impairment caused by brain damage.* Student 4: Okay, what happened to this person that caused brain impairment? Student 12: *(reading his answer)* "A tamping rod may have penetrated Phineas Gage's skull." *The teacher joins the group.* Teacher: How was he, Julio, how was Phineas Gage different? Student 12: Because his personality changed and, and he became mad easily. (Crescenzi and Walqui, 2008)
Instructions to Students: A Letter from the Teacher Dear Class, After the work we did yesterday, I started to think about the linguistics book I am asking you to write. I thought that it might be more interesting for you to write and read if we wrote the book as a series of letters to someone. So, instead of writing this as a textbook, think of these five chapters as a series of letters to tell someone what you are learning about language. You can talk about the problems you are having, about things we are doing you like and do not like. Be yourself...	*A student reads to the class from his completed assignment.* Student: First of all I think that language is a way to inform others around you your feelings or just a simple thing that you want to let know people what's the deal. And it can be expressed by saying it, watching a picture, or hearing it, you know what I'm saying? I don't know if you have heard about the kangaroo rat that stamps its feet to communicate with other rats. It's really funny cause we humans have more characteristics to communicate to each other, but we still have problems to understand other people. Characteristics like sound, grammar, pictures, and body language are some of it, while the rat only uses the foot. *(slaps the tabletop in imitation of the kangaroo rat)* (DeFazio and Walqui, 2001)

Figure 5. Sample Student Experiences with Different Genres *(continued)*

Text	Student Work
Geometry Blackboard Aim: Are there shortcuts to determine if 2 triangles are similar, as there were when we were trying to determine if 2 triangles were congruent?	*(Following a student's demonstration of a solution involving similar triangles, a classmate asks a related question.)* Student 5: Can you tell whether a polygon is similar to another one because of the angles, around it, or only because of the sides? Teacher: What does it mean to be similar? Do you remember? *(writes "Similar —" on the board.)* Student 5: I think alike in some way. Teacher: They are alike in some way. They're not the same, but they are alike. How are they alike? What does similar mean? Student 6: They have the same shape and, uh Teacher: Okay, same shape and what else? *(writes "same shape.")* Student 6: Uh, gosh, oh — and the same angles. Teacher: Okay, good. Same, or congruent, angles. *(writes "same (congruent) angles.")* And what has to be true about their sides? Luz? Student 7: They are in proportion. Teacher: *(Writes and repeats)* And sides are in proportion. *(points to completed statement: "Similar — same shape, same [congruent] angles, and sides are in proportion")* That's what it means. (Gonzales and Walqui, 2004)

Culture, Language, and Identity

In the classroom, we need to remember at all times that we are educating whole persons, not just language-processing and language-producing automatons engaged in "input crunching," as Richard Donato terms it (1994, p. 34). Learning a language is not merely a matter of studying grammar and vocabulary and practicing the skills of reading, writing, speaking, and listening. Language is learned primarily in the process of developing a "voice" in the language, an ability and desire to be heard while claiming the right to be listened to.

The Identities of English Language Learners

How are culture, language, and identity related? What is the role of language in the identities of English language learners?

English language learners commonly come to school with a cultural background relating to their home country or the home country of their parents and grandparents. There are many different ways that this cultural identification is perceived — by the school, by the students themselves, and, indeed, by their families and neighborhoods. As learners growing up, they interact within their family, in the neighborhood, at school, and, possibly, in other places as well, such as online social websites or after-school worksites. In each of these places, they need to present themselves in somewhat different ways and are constantly required to make accommodations, change the way in which they position themselves, negotiate with others about their rights and duties, and so on. Parents may insist on one appellation, peers another, teachers and institutions yet another. At a most basic level, a Korean teenager may wonder, "Am I Korean, American, or Korean-American?" Some students are insistent on maintaining their family's cultural identity and home language, their *L1*; others are rather ambivalent about it or even feel a sense of shame.

Add to this the complexities of learning the second language, the *L2*, and it should be no surprise that these learners face many challenges. As one sociolinguistics researcher, Bonnie Norton Peirce, observes, identity is a site of struggle (1995). However, in order to gain proficiency in English, English language learners must develop L2 identities. This is not an automatic or easy process.

Students' perceptions of how the majority culture accepts or rejects the culture and language they bring to school are extremely important for their eventual success (Cummins, 1984; Skutnabb-Kangas, 1984; Suárez-Orozco, C., Suárez-Orozco, M., and Todorova, I., 2008; Verhoeven, 1990). In a climate where English language learners' culture and language are validated through class practices, these learners can develop a positive academic identity because they will be valued and listened to as "speakers in their own right" (Kramsch, 1993). They will have the "right to speak" (Norton Peirce, 1995) in class, and even though their participation may be "peripheral" at first, it is always "legitimate" (Lave and Wenger, 1991).

Michael Agar argues that the relationship between language and culture is so intertwined as to require the term "languaculture" (1994). Agar points out that, for much of the twentieth century, linguists built a wall around language, assuming it to be a self-contained system held together by internal relations and rules. Schools have often taught this "walled language" without much connection to such real-world systems as those of culture, history, social relations, identities, work, and leisure. Language skills have often been practiced separately, and grammar and vocabulary have been regarded as fixed bodies of knowledge, to be studied in their own right. Indeed, there is disagreement even about whether students' study of their second language must be "walled off" from their first language, about whether L1 use is *detrimental* to the development of L2.

The L1–L2 Connection

What is the role of L1 in learning L2? In what ways does L1 support or compete with acquisition of L2?

What is it like to learn two (or more) languages at the same time? It is commonly believed that these languages will interfere with one another, causing a jumbled mix of pieces from this and that language, thereby causing constant communication difficulties. This belief influences education policies for immigrant children, the upshot being that the promotion of L2 is widely perceived to require the abandonment of L1, and time spent on L1 is commonly perceived to be time wasted that could have been used more profitably to study L2, and so on.

Do languages really compete with each other, or is there a more complex relationship? The answer depends on whom you ask. In the first part of the twentieth century, when behaviorism was the dominant psychological theory and language was seen as a set of habits, it was, indeed, assumed that if there was a difference between the habits of two languages, the habits of L1 would interfere with the habits of L2. In addition, it used to be claimed quite often that early bilingualism caused a variety of problems, including bedwetting, stuttering, and retarded language development.

However, research in subsequent years has demonstrated that bilingualism has significant positive effects in terms of cognitive flexibility, intercultural skills, and identity development. As for the effects of "competition" between two languages, while there often is some negative transfer from L1 to L2, there is also positive transfer, and by and large the positive influences of L1 far outstrip the negative ones. For example, the indisputable fact that learners will inevitably compare and contrast L1 and L2 mentally as they struggle to understand patterns and expressions does not mean that the two (or more, in some cases) languages compete in the brain. Rather, it means that the learner is working hard to become what British researcher Vivian Cook (1995) calls a "multicompetent language user," a person who controls multiple language resources and can use one language to shed light on another. Many other researchers have found very similar results. For example, Marta Antón and Fred DiCamilla (1988) investigated classes of learners of Spanish as a foreign language and found that learners used their L1 mainly for the following three reasons:

- moving the task along (structuring, planning, and explaining the task to each other);

- focusing attention on and talking about aspects of L2 that cause problems; and

- interpersonal interaction (social and affective issues).

In general, of course, teachers prefer it when English language learners use English during task work. As in the example below, however, it is typical that L1 plays *some* role during activities in L2:

> *Having read a case study of brain damage, group members work together to answer a question.*
>
> Student 9:   How 'bout a spike through the brain? It just says, "What happened to this person to cause brain impairment?"
>
> Student 14:   It's right here. Isn't it this? *(underlines a phrase in the text, which group members reject)*
>
> *Then Student 12 returns to Student 9's idea.*
>
> Student 12:   ¿El tubo que se metió? [The rod that penetrated?]
>
> Student 9:   Sí, aqui. [Yes, here.] That's what I think.
>
> (Crescenzi and Walqui, 2008)

In this instance, we see students use L1 to compare academic language in English and Spanish and then as an expression of an apparently collegial atmosphere.

Studies have also found that as L2 proficiency increased, the use of L1 naturally decreased (see for example, Brooks, Donato, and McGlone, 1997; Swain and Lapkin, 2000). A survey by Turnbull and Arnett (2002), published in the *Annual Review of Applied Linguistics,* reviews many such studies. Overall, research in this area suggests that although L2 use should be encouraged, the use of L1 can in many cases be a positive factor. There is no empirical research showing that banning L1 from the learning context is beneficial, although there is evidence that prohibiting its use can be detrimental.

To suggest another way L1 can be beneficial, we would like to cite a small study that a graduate student conducted some years ago (Fleming, 1994). At that time, she was sharing an apartment with a fellow student. The student doing the study (Fleming) spoke English and Spanish, but her roommate spoke only English. A young Argentinean man who spoke Spanish and English was visiting the area and became friends with both of them. Fleming decided to make an audio recording of a conversation in English between herself and the Argentinean and of another conversation, necessarily in English, between her roommate and the Argentinean. She transcribed both conversations and compared and analyzed the language used in them. She also interviewed the Argentinean afterward to ask which conversation went better.

It turns out that the conversation with Fleming contained some Spanish here and there, as well as some cultural references to Spanish-speaking countries and people, whereas the other conversation, of course, contained only English and very few specific cultural references. Most interestingly, in the conversation with Fleming, the Argentinean's language use was much richer: the English was more fluent and more complex and there were more topic changes and instances of trying out new constructions. In addition, both speakers participated equally. During the interview, the Argentinean commented that he had felt more comfortable in the conversation with Fleming because using Spanish now and then "lubricated" the conversation and he felt freer to discuss all sorts of topics. In the conversation with the roommate, the L2-only conversation, he often felt hesitant to contribute and, basically, just answered questions and followed the topics initiated by the native-speaking interlocutor.

While a small study like this doesn't, of course, prove anything, it should alert us, as teachers, that there is a legitimate role for L1 in the L2 classroom. So, rather than "banning" L1 use, teacher and students alike might be well advised to monitor their L1 and L2 use and reflect on instances in their lessons when L1 is useful and when it is not.

Language and the Brain

Language learning is social, and it is also cognitive. The sociocultural perspective that QTEL advances maintains that the social and the cognitive are inextricably bound together and that cognitive processes develop through rich, challenging, and well-supported activities. In this section we will look at the relations between cognitive and social aspects of activities.

Schema and the Experiential Basis of Cognition

In the case of English language learners, why are schema building and bridging to learners' experiences important?

There are many theories about language and cognition that try to explain how language is processed and how it is represented in the brain. We cannot review all of them at length here, yet there are some well-established cognitive characteristics that are of crucial importance in learning a second language. One of these is information-processing theory and, as part of this, the notion of schema and script; another is the experiential basis of cognition.

Information-processing theory has led to many useful advances in knowledge about cognition and learning. For example, the notions of schema and script have had powerful positive consequences for the design of teaching materials. A schema refers to existing knowledge about a certain topic; a script refers to certain established sequences and steps of a particular event or activity — such as ordering food at a drive-through window or researching a topic in preparation for an essay-writing assignment. Research has shown that such prior knowledge enhances the comprehension of a specific text significantly and that just the provision or withholding of a descriptive title can affect comprehension significantly (several famous studies by psychologists John Bransford and Marcia Johnson show the dramatic effects of schema and script knowledge on comprehension; for example, see Bransford and Johnson, 1972; 1973).

A couple of short texts illustrate our point. For example, what do readers need to know to make sense of the following commentary?

> Only McCullum, who made 71 on Saturday in 186 minutes of self-denial, and Oram, whose 50 from 39 balls yesterday showed a man honing his game for the shorter battles to come, offered much to stave off a rout. But Jimmy Anderson removed McCullum last thing on Saturday and Oram was left high and dry as Sidebottom scythed irrepressibly through the tail and the England close fielders caught swallows.
>
> *(Guardian Sports,* June 10, 2008)

Clearly, readers unfamiliar with cricket will have trouble understanding what is going on here, even if they know all the words (learners might have to look up *hone, rout, scythe,* and *catch swallows* — though it's debatable how much that would help them). However, to cricket fans, it's all perfectly clear.

On the other hand, cricket fans might have trouble with the following report of a baseball game:

> Tony Clark slammed a pinch-hit, three-run homer in the bottom of the eighth inning that gave San Diego an 8-6 win over New York, and completed the Padres' four-game sweep over the Mets.
>
> *(CNN Sports,* June 10, 2008).

These two extracts use the same language — English — but to those unfamiliar with the two sports, the reports might as well be in a foreign language. Even though cricket and baseball are related sports, understanding game reports of either one requires a great deal of specialized knowledge and prior experience with the game.

Analogous to these sports examples, if English language learners are faced with texts about unfamiliar topics, they may have extreme difficulties comprehending those texts. In such cases, teachers can create scaffolding activities that increase students' knowledge and relate the texts to students' prior experiences. Giving students a list of vocabulary, such as the cricket example of *hone, rout, scythe,* and *catching swallows,* is not enough. Establishing a schema and linking (or bridging) to prior experience are far more important.

In chapter 5, we see two more detailed examples of establishing schema and bridging to prior experience. In a literature class, the teacher prepares students to understand character development by asking them to describe to a partner a time when they had to handle a difficult situation. In a psychology class, the teacher prepares students to understand behavioral manifestations of brain injury by asking them to relate to group members the outcome of an incident in which they or family members were in an accident. The English language learner below, although she begins awkwardly, contributes to her own and her group's understanding of "behavioral manifestation":

> When I was seven I had seen my cousin got burned with fire. Her entire body was wrapped around her veil and when she turned the stove off that was burning with fire, her veil got caught and she got burned. She was known to be very quite fashionable and very happy-go-lucky kind of person, but after that she was very quiet and less talkative. She had a little shock about it.

> (Crescenzi and Walqui, 2008)

As this student's contribution suggests, language is not stored separately in the brain in the form of lists of words or grammatical rules. The experiential basis of cognition means that recalling past experiences helps to integrate new experiences (such as those contained in academic texts) and prepares the learners to move from informal narratives to academic reports. In this second example from the lesson on brain injury, the teacher alerts the student to the precise language connecting his experience and one in the upcoming text:

Student 11: Well, he said that like sometimes when he hears the motorcycles or something he has like twitches or stuff and like yeah.

Teacher: Yeah, so he gets twitches when he hears certain sounds?

Student 11: And he hears stuff.

Teacher: Say that again?

Student 11: He hears stuff that other people don't sometimes.

Teacher: Do you remember what that's called in psychology?

Student 11: You said auditory something.

Teacher: Yeah, what's it called? Um, hello, not a technical term. Germán, do you remember what that's called when somebody hears things that aren't really there?

Student 9: Nah.

Student 11: I told him auditory something.

Teacher: Auditory something. Auditory means he hears it. What's the word for something that's not really there? Begins with an "h." *(Several students guess.)*

Teacher: Yeah. Hallucination. Good. So his uncle now has auditory hallucinations. So he hears things that aren't there and nobody else hears, but are they, they're completely real to him. As opposed to visual hallucinations where you see things that aren't there. And I'm glad you brought that up because one of our famous people because of their brain damage will have similar [reactions]. Some people believe she has auditory hallucinations.

(Crescenzi and Walqui, 2008)

As we can see, strong connections can be fostered between personal experiences and academic topics on the one hand and between informal narratives and academic descriptions on the other. In various activities illustrated in this book, teachers use students' stories and discussions as scaffolding for the transition to academic language, and this includes moving from talking to reading and writing. In this way, promoting students' cognitive functioning is not a matter of "drumming" things "into their heads" or exposing learners to a lot of input, but, rather, of having them work collaboratively to achieve higher levels of understanding — and to appropriate academic language along the way.

Multimodal Discourse and Multisensory Learning
How can a text be scaffolded by using various resources outside the text itself, and how does this involve all the learner's senses?

In the discussion of schema and the experiential basis of cognition, we saw that using language in context relies on more than just language in the narrow sense of words and sentences.

Discourse, or the use of language in connected texts and contexts, is multimodal; it relies not only on linguistic signs pure and simple, but also on images, lines, drawings, arrows, gestures, colors, sounds, intonation, stress, rhythm, movement, and so on, in an infinite array of possible combinations.

Whenever a listener or reader has a problem interpreting a particular phrase or utterance, the usual strategy is to appeal to extralinguistic factors. For example, if someone says, "Well!" how do we figure out what he means? Obviously, we look at the person, evaluate his facial expression, posture, and direction of gaze, scan the surroundings for clues, and so on. Purely linguistically, we would never crack that word "Well!" in terms of its meaning, then and there. We need various clues from the environment to determine that, in this case, the person who's looking out the window at a cold and gloomy street in Moscow, means, "Well! Here we are, in May, and it's just started snowing again. I'm fed up with this lousy weather!!" (this example is adapted from Voloshinov, 1973; see van Lier, 2004, p. 111).

Sometimes textbook materials or lessons make the mistake of assuming that the nonlinguistic elements are just decorations, icing on the communicative cake. The whole point of nonlinguistic elements should be to *add* meaning. When treated as "icing," such decorations not only fail to support or amplify readers' understanding of the text, but also can actually confuse or distract readers from the intended focus.

If language is multimodal, it follows that language learning is multisensory. In other words, language learning involves all the senses, not only seeing (in the case of written language) or hearing (in the case of spoken language), but both and, in addition, touch, movement, and even smell (in the case of memories, for example) and taste (when exploring the connections between language, food, and culture). In fact, research into language, language development, cognition, and social psychology increasingly points to the whole-body, or embodied, nature of learning and cognition. The brain does not do all the work on its own, and language is not stored in terms of rules, words, and meanings, but in terms of experiences. In cognition, as in action, language is part of the wider realm of emotion, participation, experience, and engagement (Gibbs, 2005).

Accuracy and Fluency

What are some ways that English language learners encounter the accuracy-fluency, form-function tension inherent in learning a new language?

In language education, it is safe to assume that *accuracy,* the use of correct forms, and *fluency,* the fluent and effortless expression of ideas, are of equal importance. At the same time, it is not easy to get the balance right in particular classroom activities, especially when English language learners are struggling with ever more complex concepts and subject matter. A constant tension in a teacher's language development work with English language learners is to reconcile a dual concern with accuracy and fluency. This involves frequent shifts from focus on meaning to focus on form.

The accuracy-fluency (also known as form-meaning or form-function) distinction is one of the most pervasive dichotomies of language. We tend to look at language in one of two ways: either as a collection of words, rules, sentences, and so on or as a vehicle for conveying meaning. It seems as if we see one or the other, but not both at the same time. In that sense, it is a bit like the psychological trick pictures that, depending on how you look at them, are either one thing or another, a witch or a young girl, for example, or a rabbit or a duck (see figure 6).

Our vision can switch from rabbit to duck, but we cannot see the rabbit and the duck simultaneously — it is either the rabbit or the duck, not both at the same time.

So it is with language. Either we focus on the forms (sounds, letters, words, phrases), or we focus on the meaning. Too much of a focus on form might interfere with the meaning, whereas when we focus on the meaning, we tend to ignore the

Figure 6. A Question of Focus

Source: Wikimedia Commons (Jastrow, 1899).

forms. In everyday life, when native speakers communicate, the focus is mostly on meaning; it only switches to form when something goes wrong, for example, when an interlocutor makes an error or communication breaks down in some way. In a second-language context it is similar, except that learners might focus on form more frequently because they are struggling with the construction of linguistic messages.

In classroom work, we can often see such switches between focus on form and focus on meaning. Here is a brief example from an ESL class in a Florida middle school:

> [The teacher] stood in front of her middle-school students...and asked them what was on her feet.
>
> "Sleepers?" offered one seventh grader.
>
> "Not sleepers. If it's a short 'I,' what do you have to do?" explained the ESOL teacher, emphasizing the difference in pronunciation between slippers with an I and sleepers with two E's.

> (*Miami Herald,* December 26, 2008)

The first thing to note is that the teacher switches here from a focus on meaning (what's on her feet) to a focus on form (the correct vowel sound). We do not know if this was a form-focused activity about vowel contrasts or a meaning-focused activity about wearing slippers in the house and rubber boots in the muddy street, but we will leave that aside, noting simply that the concern at this point is with accuracy, rather than fluency.

When focusing on accuracy, the teacher's knowledge about language comes into play. The difference between "EE" and "I" is a problem for Latino students (as well as for speakers of other languages that do not have separate phonemes for these two sounds — Japanese, Arabic, French, and many others). This is a problem in speaking as well as in reading, for two different reasons. In speaking, such L1 speakers do not hear the difference between those two vowels, since in their L1 such a difference does not exist. In reading, the problem is that the two sounds are not consistently represented by the same graphemes. This means that the teacher must have linguistic knowledge in order to deal with these formal issues with these L1 speakers.

The message here is that explicit knowledge about linguistic features can be very useful for learners, but we have to be careful how to analyze the problem and how to phrase and present that knowledge. We are not suggesting that the middle-schoolers in the example above should have received a phonological lecture. In fact, even the teacher's citation of the "short I" rule may have been of no use to the students. Perhaps, in this example, the best advice for a teacher would be to tell the students that it is perfectly natural for them to confuse "EE" and "I" since their L1 doesn't have both of these sounds. When the teacher explains this, the learners can understand why they have a particular problem and then more readily recognize and begin to solve it.

The above example argues for a solid basis of linguistic knowledge for teachers of English language learners so that they understand the nature of errors students may make and the nature of the feedback that will actually be useful. Such feedback should not be derived from abstract linguistics books or isolated rules. Rather, it should come from the teacher's knowledge about language and language learning, in combination with the teacher's knowledge of the students and their learning strategies, styles, difficulties, and goals. Decisions to focus on form should arise from actual examples of classroom language use and an analysis of errors and error treatments on the basis of such data.

In addition, academic proficiency relies not only on precise and sometimes complicated grammar rules but also on a set of formulaic expressions that students may first learn simply to move assignments along ("That reminds me of...," "I agree with...," "I think the story is about ...," and so on; see Ellis, 2008). Such phrases can be modeled and practiced and can be made available as charts, handouts, or wall posters. This is not to suggest that formulaic expressions can replace paying attention to grammatical structures, but, rather, that they allow for an increase in fluency while promoting a gradual improvement in grammatical accuracy. Formulaic expressions are relatively fixed and stable, and they can be used confidently and reliably, giving learners a sense of security. Yet, at the same time, they can be varied and adapted to different situations, and gradually they can be analyzed in terms of their grammatical properties and then expanded into increasingly different options. So, for example, "I agree with" could become "I think I agree with," "I agree more or less," and so on. Little by little, more-varied grammatical choices become available, and in this way, the learner's fluency and accuracy develop.

One important variable in the accuracy-fluency mix is that of *complexity.* When English language learners are recounting personal experiences, they are often perfectly fluent and able to get their meanings across effectively. However, when they are struggling with complex academic subject matter, they are likely to slow down, hesitate, search for words and phrases, and focus heavily on the accurate expression of their emergent ideas. Fluency is then sacrificed to a certain degree for accuracy. This is normal, and it happens to all of us when we need to get across difficult ideas for the first time. Gradually, fluency increases again through further experiences with the subject matter, until the next complicated issue crops up. Academic language education is thus a constant back and forth between accuracy and fluency.

Very often learners manage such accuracy-fluency transactions when they work collaboratively. While the overall focus (or goal) is on meaning, the learners have to tackle linguistic forms from time to time in order to be able to move ahead. Such episodes of focus on form have been studied in detail by Merrill Swain and her colleagues in Canada and are called Language-Related Episodes (LREs) or "languaging" (Swain and Lapkin, 2000).

The following example of languaging is from a middle school ESL class. As group members work together to write a story based on a set of illustrations, they collaboratively resolve several linguistic problems:

Student 1: *(Reading from his paper)* "They are surprised that the street is too crowded. Then they got separated in the crowd." Uh, also...

Student 2: Maybe it's better to say they got separated in the crowd while they were walking.

Student 1: *(Writing)* "While they," while they was walking...They got separated in the street... while they are walking...while they was walking.

Student 2: They WERE.

Student 1: They were?

Student 2: Yeah, W-E-R-E. Because...

Student 1: Past?

Student 3: Past tense?

Student 1: *(Reading again)* "While they were walking, while they were walking, John found ten dollar bills."

Student 3: How does it end? We need an ending. Then...

Student 1: Then... *(points to Student 2)*

Student 2: *(Reading from his paper)* "Danny was lost. He didn't know anything about the street. John was looking for Danny. Danny was very unhappy because he couldn't find John."

Student 1: How about "looks"?

Student 2: Looked.

Student 1: Looks like.

Student 2: Looked.

Student 3: I think past.

Student 2: It should be past tense because all use past tense. Looked.

Student 1: Looked.

Student 3: Looked like.

Student 1: Looked very unhappy.

(Ng and Walqui, 2005b)

In this excerpt, Student 2 recognizes the need for the plural verb form "were" to agree with the plural "we," even though Student 1 and Student 3 accept it because it is "past" and do not explicitly note subject-verb agreement. Later, Student 2 recognizes a grammatical error in the use of "looks" instead of "looked," and he again calls for consistency in the use of tense. In both interventions, Student 2 introduces an authentic reason to focus on form: with group members in agreement about the story content, their attention to form will help their audience attend to the story they have written rather than to distracting grammatical errors. The transactions these students independently make between meaning and form appear to be seamless and appropriate to their task.

Feedback and Assessment

How can teachers attend to matters of language (form and function) and content (subject matter) in an integrated fashion?

One of the most important pedagogical issues in teaching is giving feedback. Learners need to know how they are doing, and they need to receive guidance and direction. Feedback tells the learners what they are doing right and where they need to improve. Yet linguistic and affective difficulties may arise in deciding what kinds of feedback to give and how best to do so. We do not want to discourage or demotivate (or overwhelm) the learners, but neither do we want to give the impression that whatever they do or say is just fine. How do we decide what is important, and how do we balance encouragement with correction?

Figure 7, on page 74, developed by Anita Hernandez (n.d.), shows different areas of language that can be addressed in an assignment. The suggestion is that the most important areas are toward the top of the inverted pyramid

Figure 7. Feedback Priorities

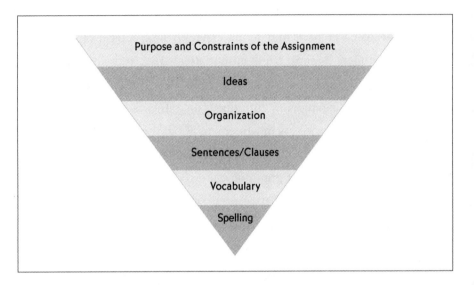

(where language meets content most closely), and the less crucial ones are toward the bottom. The message — the meaning and the content — should come first; the precision in expressing the content comes second, but it must gradually be sharpened and made more effective by fine-tuning the grammar, the vocabulary, and the discourse.

The teacher's response to an assignment should mirror its focus, whether to develop meaningful language use or to develop formal precision. In practice, however, we find that sometimes the most "red ink" is expended on the bottom areas of the pyramid, such as spelling, pronunciation, vocabulary, and grammar — even when the assignment is a first draft or journal response.

It seems reasonable that as much (or more) time should be devoted to "the big picture" as to "the small stuff." Ultimately, however, the most important job is to *connect* the meaningful and purposeful aspects of language use and its more formal aspects.

In addition to providing students with feedback on their assignments, assessments are another typical way of letting English language learners know how they are doing (and for the teacher to keep track of how the learners are doing). For this purpose, teachers can use a variety of reading and listening achievement tests and other classroom assessment tools, including self-assessments and peer-assessments, as well as teacher-assessed activities.

The purpose of such tests is *formative* rather than *summative.* They are designed to provide learners and teachers with information on how well the learners are doing and also to point the way forward to further learning. Typically, in-class formative assessments address comprehension as well as language use. However, when designing comprehension assessments for English language learners, it is important to keep in mind how difficult it can be to write questions that reveal true comprehension — that neither require prior background knowledge nor simply ask for regurgitation of the text.

Going back to the cricket report, for example, consider the comprehension questions that follow it below:

> Only McCullum, who made 71 on Saturday in 186 minutes of self-denial, and Oram, whose 50 from 39 balls yesterday showed a man honing his game for the shorter battles to come, offered much to stave off a rout. But Jimmy Anderson removed McCullum last thing on Saturday and Oram was left high and dry as Sidebottom scythed irrepressibly through the tail and the England close fielders caught swallows.
>
> (*Guardian Sports,* June 10, 2008)

1. *How did Sidebottom cause problems for the England team?*

This question requires prior knowledge of the game of cricket and the language that goes with it.

2. *What did Sidebottom do?*

To answer this question, no knowledge of cricket is required. Text can simply be plugged in directly from the report: "Sidebottom scythed irrepressibly through the tail." Anyone can answer the question without having a clue about what is going on.

3. *According to the commentator, was it a good idea to remove McCullum from the game on Saturday? Support your answer with evidence from the text.*

This can be answered by studying the text itself. Evidence includes the word "but" and the statement that "Oram was left high and dry." Further, it is reasonable to guess that "scything through the tail" and "catching swallows" might not be good for the England side.

Although question 3, above, is certainly the closest to an assessment of comprehension, for those with no cricket schema, even digging into the text to answer this question cannot clarify many other mysteries of cricket represented here. Like understanding cricket, understanding the novel and complex topics that are necessary for academic course work requires considerable work and time — in terms of building schema and bridging to students' experience and in terms of collaborative discussions and well-designed questions to understand students' comprehension successes and challenges.

In contrast to the formative assessments that are designed to inform the instruction of English language learners, we are reminded of the summative tests that label and come to stand in for the learners themselves (she's a "3," he's a "2"). Federally or locally mandated high-stakes tests such as these cannot guide learners to the goals of academic progress and success because they are not pedagogical instruments: by the time the test results come in, it is too late to build on them for day-by-day improvement.

Conclusion

To end this chapter, we draw some conclusions from the arguments presented earlier concerning the different aspects of language and apply them to actual classroom work. We are not suggesting, much less prescribing, any rigid methodology. Instead, we are proposing a flexible approach that fits the individual learner and context and is informed by an understanding of the role of language in learning and in the lives of our learners:

- English language learners need the extra support of being engaged in academic tasks that are meaningful to them and highly motivating. These learners need sustained experiences that allow them to develop an identity that includes being capable students and language users. The teacher's long-term goal in scaffolding such experiences is for students to come to see themselves as autonomous learners.

- Given the extra load of learning language and content simultaneously, English language learners need assistance in locating relevant information. Within texts, this assistance can take the form of carefully structured activities to focus learners on important information. Across texts, the design of mini-research projects and collaborative inquiries can focus learners on making meaningful connections. Such work helps learners to build and activate a schema for the subject matter at hand.

- Lesson materials must be multimodal, using visual and auditory enrichment as well as the text itself; and the work around those materials must be multisensory, employing all the senses. Texts must be read; conceptualized through illustrations; talked about in group work; interpreted through stories, dramatization, and writing; and connected to other texts and experiences.

- Both language (form and function) and content (subject matter) must be attended to, but in an integrated fashion. Teachers must be very clear about the purpose of the assignment and make sure to communicate this purpose clearly to the students.

As teachers, we may have abundant knowledge of instruction and the subject matter that needs to be taught, but much of our language knowledge is implicit: we know how to use the language, but we do not necessarily know why it is used in this or that way, the reasons for the rules of language, or the nature of the difficulties that students face. Thus, as teachers of English language learners, we must develop awareness about language and raise our consciousness about the implicit knowledge that all native speakers have. These should be crucial goals for professional reflection and development.

PRINCIPLES OF QUALITY TEACHING FOR ENGLISH LEARNERS

In defining quality teaching for English language learners (as well as for all other students), we recognize that no one size fits all. The definition of quality teaching must account for the many and diverse ways of teaching that can address students' needs with excellence. Teacher A may do it differently from Teacher B, but both teachers will have met important criteria while responding to the particular contexts in which each is teaching. All good teaching is situated in the particular — it responds to the specific students and their specific circumstances, while keeping the intellectual rigor constant. Accordingly, in this chapter we propose five principles that help us understand and define excellent teaching:

- Sustain academic *rigor* in teaching English learners
- Hold high *expectations* in teaching English learners
- Engage English learners in quality teacher and student *interactions*
- Sustain a *language focus* in teaching English learners
- Develop a quality *curriculum* for teaching English learners

Principles: The Cornerstone of Practice

How can being explicit about our teaching theories lead us to improve our teaching?

Why focus on theory and principles as our starting point? Some might object that this is an abstract place, far removed from the daily concerns and challenges of the classroom. We would argue, however, that carefully elaborated principles are actually the cornerstone of informed practice.

It has been said many times that all teachers have a theory of teaching and learning — beliefs, and actions consistent with those beliefs, that help them plan and teach their lessons. The trouble is, this theory may be implicit or explicit. If it is implicit, our theory influences our teaching, but we are not able to give a clear, precise, or consistent answer to the question "Why are you teaching in this or that way?" Thus, an implicit theory may stand in the way of continuous improvement and reflection. However, if our theory is explicit, we can talk about it, elaborate on it, and evaluate and redirect our own teaching by referring to it. We are more likely to be able to rationally defend the way we do things, continuously seek to improve our practice (and refine our theory), and engage fruitfully with other teachers in discussions about what constitutes "good teaching." We will then also come to realize that "good teaching" is not some fixed abstract property that applies in the same way across diverse contexts, but that, in fact, it is always situated in the particular.

The principles presented here have been abstracted from hundreds of reflective observations of teaching in middle and high schools in this and other countries. They emerged from our effort to distill from the specific what was constant across classes in which students' potential and diverse conceptual, linguistic, and cognitive skills development was advanced in profound and accelerated ways. Although they define the terrain of good teaching in a specific way, these principles are consistent with and overlap those of others whose work we respect, for example, the Institute for Learning's *Principles of Learning* (Resnick, Hall, and Fellows of the Institute for Learning, 2006).

These principles elaborate our theoretical understandings that student development is a consequence of (and not a prerequisite for) carefully planned opportunities for students to participate in meaningful and demanding academic activity with others and that learning is primarily a social and cultural, rather than individual, phenomenon. Figure 8 shows how these principles could be enacted in terms of classroom goals and objectives. Following Graves (1996),

> [Goals are] general statements of the overall, long-term purposes of the course. Objectives express the specific ways in which the goals will be achieved. The goals of a course represent the destination; the objectives, the various points that chart the course toward the destination. (p. 17)

Principle One: Sustain Academic Rigor

In its specifics, how does the definition below of academic rigor match your experience and your current instruction?

The fact that learners are learning English does not mean they are incapable of tackling complex subject matter concepts in this new language. Indeed, the main purpose of this book is to show ways teachers can support English language learners to access and engage with high-level subject matter content while sustaining academic rigor. To restate Principle One colloquially: Do not dumb down the academic challenge for English language learners, whether in social studies, English, math, science, or any other subject.

Figure 8. Principles of Quality Teaching for English Language Learners, with Goals and Objectives

Principles	Goals	Objectives
Sustain Academic Rigor	Promote deep disciplinary knowledge	Develop central ideas in the discipline first, postponing interesting but secondary details
		Establish interconnections among central ideas of the discipline
		Deepen understanding of themes over time
	Engage students in generative disciplinary concepts and skills	Have students anchor new knowledge to central concepts to build understanding
		Have students apply familiar central ideas or strategies to their emerging understanding of new concepts
		Invite students to build increasingly complex explanations of disciplinary concepts and processes
	Engage students in generative cognitive skills (higher-order thinking)	Have students combine facts and ideas to synthesize, evaluate, and generalize
		Have students build arguments, solve problems, and construct new meanings and understandings
Hold High Expectations	Engage students in tasks that provide high challenge and high support	Provide students with activities that are robust, but flexible enough to allow multiple entry points: all students, regardless of where they start, will benefit from participation
		Scaffold students' ability to participate in the activities
		Ensure that students are asked to engage in increasingly more complex tasks
		Treat students proleptically — as if they already possess the abilities you are seeking to develop (see chapter 2)
	Engage students (and teacher) in the development of their own expertise	Conduct metacognitive activities so that students gain knowledge of how to learn, how to monitor their progress, and how to self-correct
		Provide practice in the use of academic tools and activities so that students appropriate them over time
		Encourage students to support each other in their development
		Encourage students to support each other in building academic stamina
	Make criteria for quality work clear for all	Use rubrics to spell out expected quality of work
		Encourage students to take risks and to work hard to master challenging academic work

Principles	Goals	Objectives
Engage Students in Quality Interactions	Engage students in sustained interactions with teacher and peers	Invite students to go beyond brief, single responses and to elaborate, illustrate, and connect to their interlocutors' ideas
	Focus interactions on the construction of knowledge	State explicitly that constructing new understandings is hard work, that it requires listening intently to interlocutors, making sense of what they are saying, and deciding how to respond, either by agreeing and providing further evidence or by disagreeing and stating why this is the case Ask students to focus on the coherence of what they are saying (Are they staying with the main ideas? Are they making sense?) and to deepen their understanding by making connections to related ideas
Sustain a Language Focus	Promote language learning in meaningful contexts	Provide explicit examples, for example, formulaic expressions, of how to mark agreement, disagreement, and other moves in response to an interlocutor or text
	Promote disciplinary language use	Focus on the social purpose of genre, audience, structure, and specific language of disciplinary texts; have students practice deconstructing and creating similar texts
	Amplify rather than simplify communications	Give rich and varied examples, looking at difficult concepts from several angles
	Address specific language issues judiciously	Focus corrective feedback on fluency, complexity, or accuracy, but not at the same time
Develop Quality Curriculum	Structure opportunities to scaffold learning, incorporating the goals above	Set long-term goals and benchmarks Use a problem-based approach with increasingly interrelated lessons Use a spiraling progression Make connections between subject matter and students' reality Build on students' lives and experiences

The first goal that flows from this principle is *to promote deep disciplinary knowledge*. This notion of deep knowledge is the opposite of superficial knowledge, which focuses on atomistic recall and inert facts. Too often, large-scale standardized tests, which favor easily measured superficial knowledge, lead to a school culture that emphasizes frequent testing and quantification of factual recall and similar data that are readily captured. While factual knowledge can be very important, this is true only to the degree that learners understand if, when, and how the facts are relevant — how facts interrelate and how to use them to solve real-life problems.

To achieve deep disciplinary knowledge, learners must be supported to understand key ideas in a subject area, the deep connections between and across facts related to those core ideas, the basic conceptual structure of the discipline, the processes valued in the field, and the preferred ways of expressing them. This kind of search for integration and connection has been uncommon in teachers' own training and practice (see for example Cohen, 1988). As Richard Elmore suggests,

> Most teachers tend to think of knowledge as discrete bits of information about a particular subject and of student learning as the acquisition of this information through processes of repetition, memorization, and regular testing or recall. (1996, p. 2)

Many teachers, then, must critically reflect on their own experiences as learners, reconceptualize disciplinary knowledge, and rethink how to support students' understanding of core disciplinary ideas and processes. Teachers' solid knowledge of the subject matter must be complemented with *pedagogical* subject matter knowledge (Shulman, 1987) — knowing how to socialize the learners into the discipline. For example, teachers apprentice learners into how to weave deep interconnections in a discipline, first by modeling the process for them and then by providing students with opportunities to explore the significance of central themes over an appropriate period of time. Teachers further support this process by connecting these themes with what happened before in the curriculum and what will be undertaken next. Teachers sustain academic rigor by keeping the focus clear: main themes appear time and again, as *leitmotifs,* and each time they reappear, students' understanding should deepen.

Two other goals for sustaining academic rigor — *to engage students in generative disciplinary concepts and skills* and *to engage students in generative cognitive skills (higher-order thinking)* — can be illustrated with a simple example. English language learners need to be invited to combine ideas, to synthesize, to compare and contrast, and so forth. It's true that, in many cases, they may not have the language to do so on their own, but if provided with useful expressions and carefully guided choices, they can begin to apprentice into the language and make sense of the concepts. This should happen even in the beginning ESL class. If students can say, "This is a square" and "That is a triangle," they can also be helped to understand and say, "This figure is a square because it has four sides, and that figure is a triangle because it has three sides."

The idea that teachers can focus their instruction on central ideas and deepen students' understanding over time brings to mind an issue that teachers commonly raise: "I cannot teach everything in the curriculum." An appropriate response to this tension is: *nor should you.* In his long career as an education reformer, Ted Sizer steadfastly maintained that in education, "less is more." Applied to the principle of sustaining academic rigor, this means that teachers judiciously select substantive and generative concepts and skills to focus on with students. If students understand the central concepts that make up the core of a discipline and the main ways these concepts are interrelated, they will then be able to anchor and build other understandings; they will generate new knowledge.

Principle Two: Hold High Expectations

In what ways can differentiation support high (rather than different) expectations?

Readers may be familiar with the classic study of the "Pygmalion effect" (Rosenthal and Jacobson, 1966). In this study, teachers were given a list of students whose IQ tests supposedly showed they were about to enter an intellectual "spurt"; teachers paid more attention to these more "promising" students, and the students performed better than expected. However, what the teachers did not know was that the students had been assigned to the list on a purely random basis. In other words, the differences in the students' performance were based purely on the teachers' treatment, which, in turn, was based on the teachers' expectations as derived from the fictitious list.

This study, and others like it, should serve as a powerful reminder of the influence of expectations on performance, in both the long and the short term. Such "self-fulfilling prophecies" were first defined by sociologist Robert Merton in his book *Social Theory and Social Structure*:

> The self-fulfilling prophecy is, in the beginning, a false definition of the situation evoking a new behaviour which makes the original false conception come true. (1968, p. 477)

This is a powerful and troublesome idea. If we (as individual teachers, as a school system, or as a nation) treat English language learners as incapable of succeeding academically or, worse, if we regard them as somehow deficient (lazy, unintelligent, or whatever), then these students must fight against vastly increased odds. Consider author Luis Rodríguez's recollections in *Always Running* (1993) of how school personnel treated him in high school during the 1970s. His experience may seem sadly familiar to many English language learners even today.

Friction filled the [Mark Keppel High School's] hallways. The Anglo and Asian upper-class students from Monterey Park and Alhambra attended the school. They were tracked into the "A" classes; they were in the school clubs, they were the varsity team members and letter men. They were the pep squads and cheerleaders.

But the school also took in the people from the hills and surrounding community who somehow made it past junior high. They were mostly Mexican, in the "C" track (what they called the "stupid" classes), and who made up the rosters of the wood, print, and auto shops. Only a few of these students participated in school government, in sports, or in the various clubs.

(p. 83)

The opportunity for me to learn something new became an incentive for attending Taft High School. At Keppel and Continuation, I mainly had industrial art classes. So I applied for classes which stirred a little curiosity: photography, advanced art, and literature. The first day of school, a Taft High School counselor called me into her office.

"I'm sorry, young man, but the classes you chose are filled up," she said.

"What do you mean? Isn't there any way I can get into any of them?"

"I don't believe so. Besides, your transcripts show you're not academically prepared for your choices. These classes are privileges for those who have maintained the proper grades in the required courses. And I must add, you've obtained most of what credits you do have in industrial-related courses."

"I had to — that's all they gave me," I said. "I just thought, maybe, I can do something else here. It seems like a good school and I want a chance for something other than with my hands."

"It doesn't work that way," she replied. "I think you'll find our industrial arts subjects more suited to your needs."

I shifted in my seat and looked out the window. "Whatever."

(pp. 136–137)

Despite the low expectations that defined Rodríguez's high school experiences, he was eventually able to validate his sense of himself as intellectually curious and worthy of a chance to learn. But what about learners who are less resilient? While our schools today may be less discriminatory than those Rodríguez attended, it won't be enough to swap low expectations for high expectations if we don't also provide the high levels of support that we know English language learners will need.

When a teacher we know started teaching in high school, it puzzled her to hear some teachers say, "I have very high standards for my class, that is why so few students pass it." At the time, she had not thought of a response, but that statement stuck with her. Many years later she came to understand that high challenge and high levels of support are inseparable in quality teaching. If we set high expectations for our students, we must also provide ample, deliberate scaffolding so that the promising adolescents we teach can become what they are not yet.

Providing ample, deliberate scaffolding is distinct from differentiating instruction in ways that attempt to address students' diverse needs by creating separate lesson plans for English language learners, native speakers of English, struggling readers, and so on. The QTEL approach is to differentiate within the same complex activities.[4] The goal is *to engage all students in the same tasks, designed with the same objectives, to provide high challenge and high support regardless of students' differences.* For example, a jigsaw project can be structured to involve small groups in addressing the same topic (brain function, say) with the same questions, but the subtopics

---

4   In this book we use the terms "activity" and "task" interchangeably. However, in QTEL practice there is an established difference between these terms. Activity is the general term, indicating a well-defined set of actions students performed as part of a class. Activities can be exercises or tasks. Exercises are activities that have as their main purpose the practice of linguistic items. Tasks are reserved for activities that are open-ended, where novelty emerges as students share information not previously known.

(different cases of brain injury) and level of the reading assignments can be differentiated. What is not differentiated is the task itself or the core concepts. In such a jigsaw project, every student is carefully assigned to two different kinds of groups: an "expert" group and a "base" group. First, in expert groups, students work together to become expert about their particular subtopic. Then, in base groups, students from different expert groups meet to exchange and compare what they learned.

The next chapter details how one teacher constructed such a jigsaw project for her psychology class. As she describes in the interview below, her goals were to provide multiple entry points, for students of diverse levels, so that every student's responsibility is commensurate and no group feels that they are doing work of lower importance. Rather than make random group assignments, as is common in jigsaw projects, she very deliberately "stacked the deck":

> I set up the jigsaw very, very carefully. The base groups are much more about mixing the right personalities so that the activity runs smoothly, whereas the expert groups are about ability levels.

> I assigned the base groups so that everybody would be patient with peers. In a base group, some of the students can get done a little faster, they're a little bit more cognitively aware, they have a little bit better language abilities. I make sure they're with other kids who have personalities to rein them in.

> I spent even more time structuring the expert groups. Now, I want to make it clear that every single group had college-level material, but I was still very careful. There was one reading that was significantly shorter, there was one reading that was a little bit longer but not too conceptually difficult, and then there were two that were difficult. The Phineas Gage case was the easiest one, but easy in the sense that it wasn't as long as the others. Linguistically, again, college-level material. The longest two were Stephen Hawking and Charles Whitman — and the Stephen Hawking is difficult because just understanding that his paralysis and his speech impairments don't come from what

we normally think of as spinal cord injuries, but instead come from a disease that affects the parietal lobe — that's conceptually difficult for students....So, those two cases were for my higher-level groups, and the students in the group that did Phineas Gage were all second language learners at an intermediate level of proficiency.

Stacia Crescenzi (March 24, 2008)

Regardless of students' differences in linguistic or academic strengths, in the example above, the teacher has clearly communicated by the structure of the activity that all students are considered capable of learning the same ideas and that all students are expected to grow intellectually. Conversely, giving students different tasks that do not appear to be of equal importance communicates that the teacher may not believe all members of the class community can achieve.

Mutual respect among students is essential for the smooth functioning of a class, and teachers need to actively work at promoting it. Although English language learners who are asked to participate in the same — but differentiated — tasks as their peers will likely struggle in order to make sense of complex readings and to complete the task, they will eventually get the job done, with the support of peers and the teacher. The satisfaction of persevering can become its own trigger for the development of intellectual stamina. When English language learners make errors, as they inevitably will, the errors provide opportunities to learn. As one of the authors used to repeatedly (!) tell her students, "The road to improvement is paved with errors."

It almost goes without saying that if we are going to have high expectations for students, they need to have a clear understanding of what those expectations are and the criteria by which they will be assessed. The explicitness of these criteria enables students to self-monitor and correct and, thus, to improve their own performances. Rubrics are one straightforward way to communicate expectations. Additionally, rubrics support students in developing the important metacognitive skills of self-assessment. Rubrics should not be used prescriptively, however, to curtail students' willingness to take academic risks. Some students may find that aiming always for the exact definition of success on the rubric can be self-limiting.

Principle Three: Engage English Language Learners in Quality Teacher and Student Interactions

How does problematizing instruction, as described below, support quality interactions?

Two goals flow from the principle of engaging English language learners in quality interactions. First, such interactions must be *sustained*. Students must be able to extend beyond single utterances to elaborate, illustrate, and connect to the ideas of their interlocutors. Second, the interactions must be focused on the *construction of knowledge*. These goals are, of course, related: to reach a meaningful and rich level of interaction, it is necessary for that interaction to be jointly constructed. In some instances, the interactions are between the teacher and learner; many other times, the teacher designs (scaffolding as structure) and monitors (scaffolding as process) interactions that take place among students.

Well over a century ago, linguist Wilhelm von Humboldt described expressions as having "meaning potential," a potential that is realized in interaction. To explore this meaning potential is what we want students in general, and English language learners in particular, to do: construct new knowledge by engaging in interactions that pursue understanding, enhance it, problematize central ideas,[5] propose counter arguments,

---

5   Problematization, as introduced in Paulo Freire's pedagogy, involves the learner in taking a critical stance, questioning the intent and value of central ideas: who is making a statement, why, for whose benefit, and to whose detriment. Problematization is powerful for English language learners because it carries with it a feeling of control and legitimacy.

debate, and reach some sort of conclusion. To do this, students need to listen to each other's ideas and decide whether they agree or disagree. If they agree, they may extend the other's ideas; if they disagree, they may state their disagreements and propose counter ideas. As we will see in the next two chapters, a good part of teachers' work is to construct invitations to students and to clearly lay out expectations and supports so that students can engage in these kinds of interactions.

An example of this kind of interaction comes from teacher Tony DeFazio's high school linguistics unit, which is described in chapter 6. The students, all English language learners, have been in the United States from three months to three years and range in English proficiency from beginning to intermediate. Their academic preparation is equally varied. In the class exchange extracted below, students have generated questions around their interest in language, the class has produced a composite of such questions, and students have searched for answers in a wide variety of sources provided by the teacher. On this day, students have written letters to somebody they know, communicating what they have learned about language. As students share and discuss their letters, the teacher keeps the focus on the ideas expressed and how to build arguments and coherence. Students respond directly, with evidence, to their peers' ideas:

Student 1: (*Reading from her letter*) "The parts of language are lexis, grammar, syntax, etc. The way we learn our first language is by hearing, repeating, and remembering. We learn our second language by studying, also hearing and repeating, and being in a way forced to use it if we are in another country. I found from my research that animal communication is not a language. Animal communication is different from the human communication because, in case of dolphins, they communicate through ultrasonic pulses that cannot be heard by the human ear. I don't think that there are languages better than others. This is about it, because I do not have enough time. But

I appreciate that you teach me these things and I consider you the best teacher that I ever had in my life."

Teacher: Amen, very nice job.

Class applause, general agreement, laughter

Student 2: She says that animal communication is not a language. It IS a language, that's what I think. Because they communicate with each other.

Student 1: But they don't think.

Much class reaction

Student 2: *(Initially inaudible)* A characteristic in the language, you can have words, sounds, and everything...*(inaudible)*

Student 1: But they don't have words. They don't say "mama."

Student 2: *(Initially inaudible)* In animal language are some of the characteristics that you said are there, so...it is a language.

Teacher: Julio is arguing very strongly that animal communication is a form of, is language. Lavinia's saying it's not. What do you think would be a way to help them resolve that argument in their writing?

Student 1: Similarities in the...I mean, they have sound, both of them. Because we have sound and animals have sound, but they don't have lexis, they don't have grammar.

Much class reaction

Student 3: I hear people say that animals, they understand everything, but only thing they don't do is, they don't speak. So, that's the only thing (inaudible) they understand like humans do.

Student 4: Look, if you want to say, "Excuse me" *(makes sound of clearing his throat to demonstrate that sounds can replace words to communicate),* "huh, huh."

Student 1: They don't say, "Excuse me."

Student 4: Same thing, sound.

Much class reaction

Teacher: Hold on, hold on. Angela has something.

Student 5:	What I want to say, because they don't talk, but they communicate by doing signs, so they do not need to speak to communicate to others. So I think that's a language.
Teacher:	A lot is going to depend on how you define language, okay? You can define it in such a way as to exclude what animals do; you can define it in a very broad way, as a system of communication that includes everything. You are going to find linguists and zoologists who disagree. And if you get interested, I can give you some readings that were in the journal *Science* last year, people arguing back and forth, calling one another names because they disagreed on this issue....

(DeFazio and Walqui, 2001)

Throughout this discussion, students' sustained interactions build toward coherence and jointly constructed understanding. In summarizing the discussion, the teacher alerts students to the academic sophistication of their work together and provides a way for them to think about the origins of their arguments in the fields of linguistics and zoology. For an "observer" of this classroom excerpt, the interactions between teacher and students and among students clearly meet the definition of "high quality."

Principle Four: Sustain a Language Focus

What is the rationale for focusing on language primarily in meaningful contexts?

Teaching a class with English language learners means that every lesson, regardless of the subject area, becomes a language lesson to some extent. The teacher has to take into account that English language learners not only need to cope with the cognitive aspects of a lesson, but also will struggle with language issues — with grammar and vocabulary, listening comprehension, taking notes, and so on. Even for English language learners who have a good level of oral proficiency in everyday communication and conversation, the academic language of disciplinary discourse almost always presents problems.

As discussed in the previous chapter, however, a focus on language does not have to be in the form of grammar rules or memorization of vocabulary. Nor does it require simplification of the often-complex language of academic disciplines. The best approach to sustaining a language focus in subject matter classes incorporates three goals: *to focus on language issues in meaningful contexts and activities, to amplify students' access to the academic language they need to learn,* and *to focus judiciously on explicit language issues.*

Meaningful contexts begin at the genre level. All students should be helped to deconstruct disciplinary genres: What is the purpose of this text? What do I know about the structure of this type of text? What tends to come first, follow, and then conclude it? What patterns of academic language use are typical (e.g., describing, explaining, justifying)? What kind of language is typical (e.g., connectors, preferred verb tenses, nominalizations)? Formulaic expressions, too, can be seen as a particular aspect of genre, as specific ways to conduct academic discussions, report laboratory findings, and present a historical claim, for example.

Teaching with a language focus also means anticipating — before coming to class but, also, on the spot in class — concepts and terms that will need to be amplified for English learners. As we saw in Tony DeFazio's linguistics class, there are many ways to gracefully communicate novel academic terms, such as "caveat" and "stipulation," for example. More important than anticipating and amplifying individual terms is amplifying learners' access to concepts, with language as the touchstone. "Short" circuits, for example, will need to be read about, discussed, drawn, discussed, constructed, discussed, and so forth.

It is not always the teacher who focuses on language in subject matter classes, of course. Learners will often take the initiative as they engage with challenging texts and activities. When they encounter particular problems that need to be resolved, they will naturally focus on language and attempt to figure out how to assign meaning and make sense of the subject matter. The teacher — and other learners — need to understand that, as we saw in chapter 3, learners can often find the solution to their linguistic problems by discussing them with each other or by utilizing targeted guidance from their teacher (see, for example, the work cited in chapter 3 by Donato, 1994; Brooks, Donato, and McGlone, 1997; and Swain and Lapkin, 2000).

Again, reprising chapter 3, the key is not to add short grammar lessons or vocabulary quizzes (although they may have some role to play in a well-balanced unit of study), but to engage learners in challenging and meaningful activities and projects and find ways of dealing effectively with the language problems that inevitably come up, in the context of those meaningful and relevant activities and projects.

A teacher's initial concern needs to be with fluency in production. If the text required is a written text, essential considerations are whether students understand the purpose of the assignment and the genre (Is this going to be an argumentative essay? a family letter? a compare-and-contrast essay? a description?). Then, the teacher needs to pay attention to whether students have ideas to present as they engage in the task of writing and whether they connect these ideas logically, building a clear argument. In a first draft, students may commit grammatical or spelling errors or they may use the same word several times. During a revision, and once the teacher is assured that students know what the intended text is supposed to do for readers, the teacher may focus on complexity. At this point, the teacher may help students combine simple sentences into complex ones by linking them with the appropriate connectors. The teacher could also invite students to look for synonyms to replace a term that has been overused. Finally, a last review will focus on the most minimal aspect of the text, spelling. Ideally, academic and linguistic work should flow seamlessly together and not constitute two separate, unrelated kinds of work.

Principle Five: Develop a Quality Curriculum

What is the necessary role of learners in the development of quality curriculum?

The principle that quality teaching for English learners requires quality curriculum necessarily draws attention to the limitations of subject matter textbooks, especially in the instruction of English learners. We are not suggesting that teachers throw out their textbooks, but it is clear that to scaffold the development of students' subject matter knowledge, cognitive skills, and language in ways described so far, the textbook can never be a complete curriculum.

Accordingly, whether teachers intend to modify, supplement, or replace textbook lessons or units, five basic design factors are particularly appropriate when developing instructional materials for English learners: (1) setting long-term goals and benchmarks, (2) using a problem-based approach (which invites students to think and act as they would in solving real-world problems) with increasingly interrelated lessons, (3) using a spiraling progression, (4) making connections between how the subject matter is relevant to the present and future lives of students and their communities, and (5) building on students' lives and experiences by drawing from the funds of knowledge that students and their communities posses. Whether anchored in textbook or teacher-designed lessons and units, quality curriculum must incorporate the learners' lives and experiences, the context in which they live, and the multilinguistic and multicultural composition of the classroom, school, and community. Such curriculum invites students to make it their own.

Once a blueprint of such a curriculum is drafted, it is important to think about how its various elements can be communicated to the students, so that they, themselves, know where they are headed and what is expected of them. In this way, they can take an increasingly active role in their development as autonomous learners.

Chapters 5 and 6 present many examples of and ideas about how to design opportunities for students to actively engage with academic content, language, and each other. We offer these examples bearing in mind our earlier proviso, that every curriculum must be designed for the specific setting in which teachers and learners live and work.

Conclusion

Five principles can be said to guide the development and enactment of quality instruction for English language learners. In shorthand, these principles call for academic rigor, high expectations, quality interactions, a language focus, and quality curriculum. QTEL has derived these principles from classroom experience; close observation of teachers and learners; sociocultural, cognitive, and linguistic theory; and research. By making these principles explicit, we, like any other educators, are able to monitor and assess our own performance, communicate about our principles with others, and modify our principles as reflection and interaction with others warrant.

We provide these principles here to make explicit the goals of the instruction that is presented in the next two chapters. In chapter 5, two teachers invite us into their classrooms, where they are apprenticing QTEL approaches to instruction and curriculum design. In chapter 6, unit and lesson design are explored in even more deliberate detail.

PEDAGOGY IN ACTION
THE APPRENTICESHIP OF TWO TEACHERS

The development of teacher understanding, very much like the development of student understanding, occurs as a result of opportunities to participate in a wide variety of activities — sometimes in collaboration with others, sometimes individually. For teachers, the focus of such activities is to reflect on and refine their subject matter knowledge, lesson planning skills, and classroom practice. In this process, they build continuously on their current state of knowledge, incorporating new ideas and skills and revising and challenging concepts that are inconsistent with recently developed understandings.

In this chapter, we observe two teachers,[6] in very different contexts, whose ongoing apprenticeship into QTEL practices is reflected in carefully scaffolded lessons of their own design. These are accomplished teachers who nevertheless are participating in professional development to increase their effectiveness in ESL and mainstream classrooms with widely diverse students, using QTEL task structures to set up opportunities for each student's individual growth.

---

6   The teachers featured in this chapter have chosen to have their real names used, rather than pseudonyms.

Two Contexts

How do these teachers' goals for their own professional development relate to the QTEL principles described in chapter 4? What social, emotional, and academic differences can they expect to see between first-generation and second-generation English language learners? How might these differences affect their instructional decisions?

Roza Ng, an 18-year veteran teacher, teaches at Middle School 131 in the area of New York City known as Chinatown. About 85 percent of the school's 900 students have a Chinese background, about a third are English language learners, and 90 percent are low-income, based on their qualification for free or reduced-price lunch. The school has a comprehensive bilingual program, and when students who are English language learners first arrive, they are placed in ESL classes and, also, take subject area courses in Mandarin or Cantonese. Once they reach an intermediate level of proficiency in English, they are mainstreamed into English-only classes. In the class we visit, all of Ng's students are first-generation immigrants to the United States. Their literacy levels in their first language (Chinese or Spanish) run the gamut from low to very accomplished, but, as newcomers, almost all are eager to learn English and the academic skills required to succeed in the United States.

Stacia Crescenzi, formerly a community college teacher and now an assistant principal at Lanier High School in Austin, Texas, teaches the second class we will visit, an elective psychology course. Of the 1,800 students at Lanier, 70 percent are Latino, 39 percent are English language learners, and 90 percent qualify for free or reduced-price lunch. Crescenzi's class is a mixture of native English speakers, first-generation English learners, and several second-generation English language learners whose command of English is not proficient for academic work, even though they were born in the United

States and have attended American schools exclusively. Many of these students, having experienced failure and tracking throughout their schooling, internalize oppositional patterns of behavior in response (Csikszentmihalyi and Schmidt, 1998). Unlike first-generation English language learners, who start with a clean educational slate in America and may more easily believe in the American dream, second-generation English language learners may find it difficult to believe that academic success is possible.

At the time we visit both teachers, Ng's participation in professional development is sponsored by the New York City Department of Education's three-year partnership with QTEL to train teachers and the department's professional developers in QTEL principles and approaches. In Austin, the school district is supporting two of its high schools in a three-year effort to infuse QTEL practices in every classroom — mainstream as well as ESL.

Both Ng and Crescenzi, in addition to attending a series of QTEL in-service workshops, have volunteered for classroom coaching with QTEL staff members. They both are working with Aída Walqui in coaching sessions that begin with discussion of their lesson plans and include classroom lesson observations and subsequent meetings to debrief the teachers' experiences.

Three main goals motivated Ng to apprentice QTEL practices. First, while she had felt generally successful helping her students achieve, she had been a traditional teacher, teaching from the front. The students who participated were those who eagerly volunteered. For the most part, she left those who didn't volunteer alone. The results were varied, as might be expected. She could see that those who participated more seemed to accomplish more, wheras those who remained quiet did not do as well.[7] She had always

---

7 We cannot assume, of course, that quieter students are necessarily weaker students. However, it is our strong belief that designing lessons in which all students contribute helps those who are always eager to participate anyway, also helps the quiet students, and enriches the lesson as a whole.

wanted to help the quiet students speak more in class. She knew better than to concede the stereotype of the quiet Chinese student, since she could hear these same "quiet" students talking excitedly in Chinese during breaks and at lunchtime. She wondered about what was keeping them quiet in class. Were they afraid to fail? Were they worried that if they mispronounced words or misconstrued sentences others might make fun of them? How could she turn the classroom silence into the engaging conversations that took place in Chinese outside of class?

Ng also noticed that for some of her students, failure to participate related to lack of motivation more than to feeling uncomfortable speaking English, and she wanted to change that. She recognized that active students were probably going to be more motivated students. So how could she provide them with more active, but substantive, learning opportunities?

Finally, Ng was interested in learning how to meld individual activities into fluid, coherent lessons that invited students to venture into collaborations to accomplish work they could not yet do on their own. She sometimes attempted new activities she learned from workshops or colleagues, but, even if these discrete activities worked well, she did not know how to follow up with other equally stimulating activities that would move students closer to her lesson objectives.

At Lanier High School, Stacia Crescenzi's relationship with QTEL resulted from a slightly different set of motivations. In response to what Lanier principal Edmund Oropez described as a school "teetering on becoming an 'unacceptable' school" (according to Texas standards), Oropez and his staff were looking for a professional development program that the whole school could commit to. As an assistant principal, Crescenzi had been active in deciding to have Lanier partner with QTEL in a comprehensive plan to offer high-challenge and high-support learning opportunities to all students,

especially the school's English language learners. Because Lanier adminis-
trators each teach a class as part of their duties, Crescenzi was not simply
choosing QTEL as a program to impose on others. Her own psychology
course would come under the QTEL umbrella.

Crescenzi's course is a one-semester elective that focuses on psychology
content but is also designed to boost the writing skills of students who have
yet to pass a writing test required for graduation. Her goals for the class are
at a very high level: to provide students with an opportunity to read sophisticated materials, learn to write academic essays, and, in general, become
excited about their own academic futures. Since Lanier students may enroll
in only one elective per semester and students perceive a number of other
courses as more appealing, Crescenzi found that recruiting students for the
course was not easy. When she began QTEL professional development, her
goals were to maintain her high academic expectations for students, but to
design more interactive lessons that would increase students' engagement
and, potentially, their learning.

In moving through these two classes, we will focus on the role of scaffolding (see chapter 2). At the structural level, we will see the teachers conceptualize the objectives for their lessons and the tasks that can lead students
toward those objectives. At the process level, we will observe how teachers
and students respond from moment to moment to instances of emerging
student agency.

With a focus on scaffolding, the construct of *task* becomes central. A task
may be defined as an instantiation of the pedagogical support teachers offer
students to help them accomplish their academic goals. In that sense, each
task has a specific objective for students to meet, which needs to be articulated, or aligned, with any subsequent tasks to help students eventually
reach the overall lesson objectives. A task invites students to move through

specific routines as they work at making sense of new language and ideas. It invites students to engage in predictable participation structures, and it has a clear beginning, process, and end. Familiarity with the structure of a task enables students to focus not on directions, which are especially consuming for English language learners, but, instead, on the novelty of target skills, concepts, and the language to express them. Tasks are a way for students to move economically from apprenticeship into appropriation. Each task also provides students with the opportunity to perform beyond their individual level. In task-structured collaborations, students rehearse, perform, and, eventually, own the new knowledge.

Using Tasks to Learn About Literary Character Development

In what ways does this teacher meet her larger goals of increased student talk and participation while addressing her lesson objectives? How do students respond academically and socially? What classroom climate is being built?

Roza Ng designed the particular lesson described here for her intermediate ESL class of 15 adolescents recently immigrated from China and one young man from the Dominican Republic. Students had been in the United States between six months and two-and-a-half years. Ng's lesson centers around a five-page episode from Richard Wright's memoir, *Black Boy*. In some anthologies, the excerpt is called "Hunger," because it deals with a period in Wright's childhood when his father has abandoned the family and his mother, with no money even to buy food, is forced to find work and leave Richard on his own for the first time. Ng's objective for the lesson was that students learn about character development and characterization by reading about a character they could relate to on a personal level. For class, she photocopied the excerpt so students could make annotations as they read and discussed it.

When Ng developed this lesson, she had already attended three days of QTEL professional development, where she learned — or refined her knowledge of — several tasks that she would now employ to get students interacting, with each other and with her, as they constructed their understanding of a text containing complex language and ideas. In Ng's planning session with Walqui, she outlined the task articulation she had developed to support her lesson objectives (see figure 9). The two-day lesson promised to offer many opportunities for students to speak together, varied participation structures and student groupings, and meaningful tasks to propel students toward an understanding of literary character development.

In fact, as Walqui observes Ng's lesson enactment, she can see that the class dynamics have changed.[9] Instead of participation being limited to the "usual suspects," all students are actively engaged in the activities proposed.

The lesson begins with students quietly writing some notes about one of their own experiences of having gone through a difficult situation. When it is time to exchange ideas with their partners, students who need help getting started can read the following conversation prompts, or formulaic expressions, that Ng has posted in front of class:

> Tell me about a time when you faced a difficult situation.
>
> What happened?
>
> How did you handle it?

---

8   Walqui was already familiar to the class as Ng's coach, somebody who was working with her in refining her teaching. Students were comfortable with the notion that teachers also can get support.

Figure 9. Tasks to Promote Understanding of Character Development

Lesson Objectives: Students will learn about characterization in literature, tracing the development of characters over time and providing evidence for their conclusions.	
Day 1 (45 minutes)	
Think-Pair-Share	Partners tell each other about a time when they faced a difficult situation.
Class Round-Robin	Students relate their partner's and their own difficult situations to the class.
Partner Reading and Discussion	Partners each read the text about a difficult situation, one focusing on one of the main characters and the other partner focusing on the other character. They then discuss their characters' actions and emotions.
Teacher Model	The teacher models how to record observations and evidence in the Double-Entry Journal.
Double-Entry Journal	In expert groups of four assigned to focus on one of the two main characters, students individually reread the text and make journal notes about how the character is feeling, with textual evidence to support their observations. Group members share their notes and reach agreement about their ideas and evidence.
Partner Sharing	Group members return to their original partners and exchange information about their characters.
Individual Reading	Students silently reread the text.
Collaborative Dialogue Writing	Groups of four write an extended dialogue to illuminate a particular move in the story. They practice dramatic readings of their script.
Day 2 (45 minutes)	
Collaborative Dialogue Performance	Groups perform for their classmates.
Reflection on the Double-Entry Journal	Students each review and add to or revise their journal notes based on what they learned from classmates' performances.
Mind Mirror	Groups of four create a poster that conveys in quotations, original phrases, symbols, and drawings a main character's state of mind at one point in the story.
Mind Mirror Rubric	Using a rubric, groups rate their poster and write an explanation of their rating.
Gallery Walk	Groups review the other posters created for the same character they featured. They use the rubric to write their evaluations.

As Ng and Walqui observe partnerships around the room, student interlocutors all gravitate toward the comfort provided by the formulaic expressions. Each respondent, however, then enters the task at his or her individual level of language ability. Through the varied stories partners tell, each is building a personal connection to the reading assignment that will follow, and each is developing an authentic voice in the class. In the Think-Pair-Share task excerpted below, these partners relate typical concerns of adolescence. While the boy describes his situation more fluently than the girl who is his partner, her haltingly told story of a culturally shared embarrassment elicits perfectly registered empathy.

Student 1: Tell me about a time when you faced a difficult situation. What happened? How did you handle it?

Student 2: It was a time this year. I was in the hallway, waiting to come to this class, and these seventh graders went out of the room, and my friend, Alvin, sixteen years old, pushed me and I hurt my thumb. And you? Tell me about a time when you faced a difficult situation. What happened? How did you handle it?

Student 1: It is one time in eighth grade, my report card gets an 85 on my average, so my mom yell at me. The members of my family know, and me with a sad face. I think that's embarrassed.

Student 2: *(Smiles)* It is.

(Ng and Walqui, 2005a)

After partners finish their exchanges, Ng calls on students to relate, first, their partner's story and, then, their own. In the structure of this Class Round-Robin task, each student is accountable for having listened to his or her partner, and each gets practice speaking to the class. And, for students who may be shy about broadcasting their own story to the whole group, telling their partner's story first is a relatively safe warm-up. Classmates listen with interest to learn about their peers and compare experiences. As indicated in the dialogue that follows, Ng also attends carefully and occasionally intervenes to encourage elaboration or to model correct usage and amplify vocabulary.

Student 3: The hardest thing that happened to Ray Lin was when she came to America. The first day she had to take the test in the school, and she didn't know nothing in English. She felt bad.

Teacher: Uh-huh.

Student 3: And the hardest thing I ever have to face is one time outside my old school, the old school I used to go before this one. I had a fight with, like, three people. Outside the school. I don't know why.

Teacher: Oh, boy! They just picked on you?

Student 3: Yeah. They pick on me. Every time I pass, I used to always see them like that. I always walk home, and one time they, like, jump me like that and stuff. So, I fight.

Teacher: You fought with them?

Student 3: Yeah.

Teacher: Were you all right?

Student 3: Yeah, I run very fast.

Class laughter

Teacher: After you hit them, you ran. All right.

(Ng and Walqui, 2005a)

In this brief excerpt, we see Ng accept the student's first story, about his partner, without correcting a double negative and perhaps diverting attention from the importance of his partner's experience. But when the student goes on enthusiastically to describe a situation that happened to him, Ng finds opportunities to intervene that can benefit this sturdy volunteer (and the class). She introduces the term "picked on" to synthesize his narration of an unwarranted fight and, at the same time, to encourage him to elaborate. As he goes on, she continues to demonstrate involvement with his experience, while also modeling use of the past tense. Even after the class enjoys his humorous depiction of "hit and run," Ng casually recasts it as "hit and ran."

Once students have shared their anecdotes, Ng explains why she asked them to think about a difficult instance in their lives, relating it to the excerpt they are now going to read about a difficult time in author Richard Wright's early life.

Ng instructs partners to focus each on a different main character, Richard or his mother, to underline that character's key feelings and actions, and to write their own reactions in the margins of the photocopy.

As students read, Ng moves around the room, checking their annotations and talking briefly with students about their notes or lack of them.

She then has students move to tables with others who focused on the same character. In their groups, students share their notes, reread the selection, and work on a Double-Entry Journal task (see figure 10) that prompts students to interpret how characters are feeling and provide supporting evidence for their claims.

Figure 10. Character Development Double-Entry Journal

Selected Character: _____	
How does this character think? What does he or she feel?	What is your evidence? Write down specific quotes.

Ng confers individually with groups, inviting students to share and defend their thinking. In the excerpt below, Ng picks up on a student's literal, and not incorrect, answer, but probes for deeper understanding, helping the student uncover more complex motivations for a character's behavior.

Student 4: I think Richard's mother feels tired after she finish working.

Teacher: Ah. Where in the text makes you feel that way?

Student 4: Page three.

Teacher: The first paragraph?

Student 4: Yeah.

Teacher: Can you read that?

Student 4: *(Reading from the text)* "My mother finally found work as a cook and left me and my brother alone in the flat each day with a loaf of bread and a pot of tea. When she returned at evening, she would be tired and would cry a lot."

Teacher: Ah, she was crying a lot, right? Why would you think she was crying?

Student 4: Because she miss her father.

Teacher: Ah. You think? Okay.

Student 4: *(Correcting herself)* His father.

Teacher: You mean she misses her husband?

Student 4: Yeah.

The teacher moves on, but the group carries on, digging further into the characters' emotions.

Student 5: I think Richard also humorous. Humorous. When her son ask her for food, she said she didn't tell the son directly that they didn't have any food. She said, "Go find some *kungry*,"[9] and try to make her son distract and forget the hunger.

---

9   The text (Wright 1945/1998, p. 18) reads:
"Mama, I'm hungry," I complained one afternoon.
"Jump up and catch a kungry," she said, trying to make me laugh and forget.
"What's a *kungry?*"
"It's what little boys eat when they get hungry," she said.

Student 6:   Or it could also be fear. Fear. Because after her husband gone, die, or whatever, she knew that her children were suffering hunger, and everything Richard said made her even scared. Scarier.

(Ng and Walqui, 2005a)

Having checked in with all the groups, and confident that her students understand the essence of the two characters, Ng still wants them to have a few more opportunities to use the new ideas and language, to make them their own. She has decided to try the Collaborative Dialogue Writing task she learned during QTEL in-service, having small groups re-create scenes from the reading. With that purpose in mind, she has analyzed the text and identified four key moves in the selection. She explains to students that each team of four will work on one of the scenes, drawing on the text for 70 percent of their dialogue and basing the remaining 30 percent on what they know about life. Each student will keep a full script, and after writing and practicing their scene, groups will perform for classmates the next day.

Ng assigns the following scenes:

A.   As the story begins, Richard is hungry and his mother explains why she has no money for food.

B.   Twice his mother gives Richard money to go and buy some food, and each time he gets robbed by the gang.

C.   His mother teaches Richard how to stand up for himself.

D.   Richard has no choice but to face the gang again. He handles it the way his mother taught him.

The structure of the Collaborative Dialogue Writing task orchestrates student interactions that require listening carefully to each other's ideas in order to support or challenge them and then jointly constructing lines of dialogue that represent the best thinking of the whole group. As Ng walks around the room, she listens in (and intervenes occasionally) as groups negotiate meaningful dialogue that reflects their understanding of the characters.

In the excerpt below, students are fully involved in what their characters would say to each other and *how* they would say it. As group members offer possible lines of dialogue, words get changed, improvements are introduced, and the characters' emotions are made palpable.

Student 7: *(Reading what she has written for the mother's role)* "Richard, take the money and go and buy the food. Don't dare come home without the food." *(laughs)*

Group members begin to copy the line, repeating it phrase by phrase as they do so. The line's originator comes up with a more emphatic ending after being asked to go over the line one last time.

Student 8: Can you say that again? One more? "Richard, go buy the food again." What else?

Student 7: "And don't dare to step in the house without the food."

Group members then suggest what the student reading Richard's role would say in reply. He (Student 8), however, surprises them with a pithier and more dramatic response.

Student 9: What you are going to say is that you will be very frightened and don't dare to go fight against those gangsters.

Student 7: *(To Student 8)* That's your line now. Okay? That's your line.

Student 9: *(Also to Student 8)* What are you going to say?

Student 8: "Mommy! I don't want to go!"

Group laughter. Then group members continue to coach Student 8, focusing on the delivery of the line.

Student 9: Quiet voice with fear.

Student 7: When you say your line, you are so scared.

The student playing the mother (Student 7) introduces her next line, the Richard student (Student 8) jumps in with a suggestion, but the mother student returns to her original idea.

Student 7:   My turn now. "Go now. Don't...Go now"

Student 8:   "What do you mean, you don't wanna go?!!"

Student 7:   I mean, "Go now! You must go. You must go. If not, I will beat you up."

To "temper" the response of a caring mother, Student 9 offers an alternative.

Student 9:   The mother don't say that. The mother does say, "Go now, or you will stay in the street for all night long." Something like this.

(Ng and Walqui, 2005a)

In this group, three of the four students actively participate in the dialogue negotiations, but the task structure dictates that even students who may be quieter than others must track the interchanges in order to write their own copy of a full script. The task also structures whole-group language practice, since groups must rehearse and then deliver their performances. In Ng's class, when the bell rings, a few students arrange with her to use the classroom during the lunch break to continue their rehearsals. Ng silently notes progress toward one of her goals: today, at least, these students' animated lunchtime conversations are about to be held in English.

The next morning, groups perform their dialogues in narrative order. Ng has discussed with them several different ways of having all students active during a performance, including choral reading, simultaneous pantomime and dramatic reading of the script (one student stands behind another and reads the character's lines while the student in front acts out the lines), and cuckoo-clock turn-taking (two students stand back to back, the one facing the audience reads a line, the pair rotates as if joined together, and the student who was in back is now in front and reads the next line). As the performances proceed, students clearly enjoy themselves. At the conclusion of the presentations, Ng, the whole class, and the coach appreciatively applaud this alternative version of Richard Wright's childhood experience.

To take advantage of insights prompted by the presentations, students get together in their Double-Entry Journal groups to review their earlier observations about the characters and see what else can be added. Ng comments on some of these additions and then explains that the groups will now work on a new task, called the Mind Mirror.

Ng tells her students that during a recent professional development day she very much enjoyed working with other teachers to produce a Mind Mirror for a poem they read together. Then she explains the term "mind mirror." She asks students to imagine what would happen if when they looked at themselves in the mirror, they could not see their physical features but, instead, saw their worries, concerns, feelings, dreams, hopes, and so on. She tells them that they need to imagine this kind of mirror for Richard or his mother and then capture, on group Mind Mirror posters, what the mirror would reflect. She explains more specifically what is required: To portray the character's feelings and state of mind, groups must choose two revealing quotes from the text; they will also need to create two original phrases that synthesize what the character is going through — important feelings, actions, and thoughts; they will need to choose two symbols present in the text that reinforce their presentation of the character's predicament; and, finally, they must draw two images related to the selection.

Ng distributes and discusses a rubric so that students know the criteria that will be used to evaluate their Mind Mirror. She also tells groups that before they post their Mind Mirrors, they will use the rubric to self-assess their product, offering justifications for their choice of grade (outstanding, acceptable, or needs revision).

Later, once all teams have posted their products, they evaluate the posters of those classmates who worked on the same character they did, using the rubric and sticky notes for their comments.

At the end of these two days, students have met Ng's overarching goals: the task structures she put in place demanded interaction, afforded many and varied ways to use language, and required active participation of everyone. Her particular objectives for the lesson were also met: students had demonstrated in discussion, writing, performance, and graphically that they really understood the characters of young Richard Wright and his mother and could support their ideas in the text.

Using Tasks to Understand Brain Structure and Function

In what ways does this teacher meet her larger goal of increased student engagement while addressing her narrower lesson objectives? How does this teacher's use of tasks compare with their use in the previous lesson?

In the original design of her high school psychology course, Stacia Crescenzi had organized a variety of interesting student materials for a unit about brain structure and function. She was pleased with the materials and felt that they were sufficiently sophisticated and motivating to shoulder her course's double duty of engaging students in science content while also preparing them to pass a graduation-required writing test (which they all had so far failed). Like the large majority of students at Lanier High School, most of those enrolled in her course had a Latino background, many spoke Spanish as their home language, and a number were second-generation English language learners.

After using her materials for some time, Crescenzi came to recognize that relying on the course materials to motivate her students was unrealistic and that students' learning was less than she had anticipated. She decided to revamp her unit on brain function, keeping the same materials but incorporating tasks she was learning in QTEL professional development. The tasks could structure inviting ways for students to engage with the materials and the learning opportunities she wanted her students to have.

As we visit Crescenzi's classroom, students have already begun the revamped unit. Having investigated basic brain structures and their functions, they are now exploring the behavioral manifestations of brain injury, discovering through case studies how brain function may be affected by injury to particular brain structures. The tasks Crescenzi has planned provide many opportunities for students to interact — drawing on personal connections as well as academic texts, using both conversational and academic language, and succeeding through collaboration to construct knowledge that might otherwise elude them (see the lesson plan in figure 11).

Crescenzi begins class with an explanation of the lesson objectives, which she has also outlined on the whiteboard. Her introduction, below, is clear and inviting, and she carefully sets out the notion that brain damage has "behavioral manifestations," four cases of which students will be able to compare.

> Ladies and gentlemen, by the end of this lesson you will be able to describe in detail, more detail than you could possibly imagine, one person who is famous. And part of the reason they are famous is because of their brain damage. Second thing you're going to be able to do is compare the behavioral manifestations of four different people, all of whom have brain damage. You're going to be an expert in one, but you are going to know enough about all four that you can compare them. And the main things you're going to compare are their behavioral manifestations, the actions that they do that may be a little unusual because of their brain damage.
>
> (Crescenzi and Walqui, 2008)

Before introducing the particulars of the Jigsaw Project, which is the lesson centerpiece, Crescenzi engages students with the lesson topic by asking them to consider the range of changes, some of them behavioral, that can result from an accident. She also asks them to complete a Quick-Write about a time they or someone they know had an accident.

Figure 11. Tasks to Promote Understanding of Brain Structure and Function

Lesson Objective: Students will be able to explain the behavioral manifestations of injury to specific brain structures.	
Lesson 2 (75 minutes) *	
Quick-Write	Students write about the physical and/or behavioral consequences of an accident involving them or someone they know.
Group Round-Robin	Group members take turns relating the experience they wrote about.
Anticipatory Guide	Students make preliminary judgments about controversial statements that assigned reading will confirm or refute.
Jigsaw Project	*See below.*
Individual Reading	Students each read one of four brain injury case studies.
Expert Group Discussion and Writing	Students who completed the same case study meet in groups of four to discuss the reading. Group members agree on and write answers to four questions (the same questions in all groups).
Base Group Sharing	Students meet in new groups of four, in which each member has become an "expert" on a different case study. Group members exchange answers to the four questions so that everyone has comparable written information for each case study.
Base Group Comparison	Group members discuss and write answers to questions about similarities and differences between areas of brain damage and behavioral manifestations.
Anticipatory Guide	Students reflect on and find evidence in the assigned reading to confirm or refute their preliminary judgments about controversial statements.

* Crescenzi's lesson plan schedule was optimistic. By the end of the first 75-minute class session, students had completed tasks as far as the base group sharing of notes; they completed the lesson during the next class session.

Students write for three minutes in their journals, "using complete sentences," and then relate their stories in Round-Robin groups. In the dialogue below, as students start sharing their notes in one of the groups, their differences in English proficiency become apparent. Regardless, they listen attentively to each other, and the stories contribute to their understanding of behavioral manifestation.

Student 1: Okay. It was a time that my sister was walk across the hallway [highway], then one car shock her, and then the car broke her leg. At the time she felt so bad because one month during the accident she can't walk, she shouldn't allowed. Now she's not the same girl who was last time before the accident.

Student 7: My mom was in a car accident like three years ago and probably wasn't that big but, to feel like was her fault, and she didn't want to drive, like, for one year because she said that it was her fault. So she changed. Now she will be driving, but she won't be, like, listen to music or singing like before the accident. And even though when you ask something to my mom, she won't answer if she's driving.

Student 2: Well, my cousin, he lived in Beeville, down south Texas, somewhere down by Corpus, and like me and him, we had a pretty good relationship, you know? And then like he got accepted into college and he went to San Antonio, and he was like, I don't know, he just had his own separate ways. Then one day we got a phone call that he got in an accident. And I'm like, okay, my uncle had got in an accident before, but he was okay. But he [my cousin] had like he was like in a coma for like two weeks, and he was like, he suffered from I guess from that post-traumatic stress, I guess. Now he's like real talkative. I saw him on Easter.

Student 3: Talkative?

Student 2: Talkative. Like before, he never used to talk, but he's like, he asks me like, "What's your name?"

Student 3: Oh, yeah? He'll forget?

Student 2: Yeah, and like, I knew him all my life, though, and it's sad.

Student 4: He doesn't remember you.

(Crescenzi and Walqui, 2008)

When time is up, after a short class debriefing of the Quick-Write inter-actions, students respond individually to the first part of an Extended Anticipatory Guide, a set of questions designed to elicit their opinions about content they are about to read and to generate personal reasons for reading (see figure 12).

Figure 12. Extended Anticipatory Guide: Brain Function

	Agree	Disagree	What I found out in the text
1. Each part of the brain is responsible for different functions or activities.			
2. When someone's brain is injured, he or she never recovers from the injury.			
3. The most important part of your brain is the part that controls language use.			
4. You can always tell when someone's brain is injured.			
5. People who are brain injured behave in odd ways.			

After this series of tasks to prepare her students for interacting with the lesson concepts, Crescenzi introduces the Jigsaw Project (figure 13 outlines the project structure), managing to slip in tantalizing details about each of the four case studies the expert groups will tackle.

Teacher: One of the people that we'll talk about, some people believe that she's famous because she's hearing God, and God has given her a message. And other people believe that she's hearing things nobody else hears because she had brain damage. I'll let you be the judge if you happen to be in that person's group.... [W]e have the famous Phineas Gage, who's extremely cool, because you may or may not be able to see (*shows illustration of what Gage's skull would have looked like with protruding rod*), he somehow got a pole right through his frontal lobe. Kinda cool.

Student 1: And he lived?

Teacher: Yes, he lived. We're not talking about anybody that died from their brain injuries. Very famous man. Psychologists know him really well, we learned a lot from this guy. So if you read Phineas Gage, you're going to become an expert on frontal lobe damage. Okay? Our next exciting person is the famous, currently still living, Stephen Hawking, who is a famous physicist, and he has parietal lobe damage. Remember, this is your part in your hair? So your parietal lobe is the parts of your brain on either side of your part. He's famous because he is a physicist and because of his brain damage. And one of the things, if you're in the Stephen Hawking group, I want you to think about, would he be as famous a physicist if he didn't have brain damage? ...[M]y *amygdala* group, which I just love to say, is going to be Charles Whitman, who's the guy that shot all those people from the top of the U.T. [University of Texas] tower. Oh, I see light bulbs going off everywhere.

Student 2: I thought he had a tumor, man.

Teacher: People in this group will become experts and then they shall enlighten you. That's the amygdala group.

(Crescenzi and Walqui, 2008)

Figure 13. Jigsaw Project: Structures and Functions of the Brain

Case Study 1	Case Study 2	Case Study 3	Case Study 4
Phineas Gage	Stephen Hawking	Ellen G. White	Charles Whitman

Meet in Base Groups

Students receive the assignment and meet the class-mates they will report back to as experts about one of the four articles. Each student receives a matrix with questions that apply equally to the four case studies.

Move to Expert Groups

Students join their assigned expert group, individually read the same article, confer with group members about things they did not understand, and collaborate to write answers to questions about their article — the same questions that other expert groups also answer.

Return to Base Groups

Students take turns reporting the answers their expert group has written for the questions. Students record on a matrix what they learn from each other so that each will have comparable information about all of the articles.

As we heard from Crescenzi in the previous chapter, she was extremely deliberate in assigning students to groups — creating base groups around personalities and a mix of language abilities and creating expert groups in which students' language and literacy abilities are similar. Everyone in the class participates in the same task, within base groups and within expert groups; only the length and difficulty levels of the articles assigned to the expert groups are differentiated.

Crescenzi explains the expert groups' reading task, encouraging students to read for gist and not to get bogged down in understanding every word. She points out that once students have read the assignment, they will have a chance to ask for clarification from their group members. But, as she says, "First I want you to figure out if it even matters that you understand every word."

Students have 10 minutes to work through the articles, which vary from one-and-a-half to three pages. As students near the end of their reading, Crescenzi explains the matrix that expert groups will complete for the subject of their case study. Figure 14 shows the four questions that all expert

Figure 14. Jigsaw Matrix: Damage to Lobes of the Brain

	Phineas Gage	Stephen Hawking	Ellen G. White	Charles Whitman
1. Why is this person famous?				
2. What happened to this person that caused impairment of the brain?				
3. What areas of the brain were damaged?				
4. How was this person different as a result of the damage?				

groups answer. Because students from the expert groups will go back to their base groups and share what they have written on the matrix, Crescenzi is explicit about the need for groups to agree on their answers, have a scribe write their draft answers, and, then, have the teacher approve each answer, including spelling. This ensures that individual students can copy correct information and correct English to transmit back to the base groups.

When the time comes for expert group discussion and initial agreements, students negotiate their understandings as they work toward a consensus. The following example, part of the conversation carried out by the Ellen White expert group, illustrates how students work to make sense of the reading. In this case, students do not even recognize that a concept is unclear to them until they try to write about it.

Student 5: *(Reading from her paper)* I put, "A girl threw a rock at her, hitting her in the face, which threw her brain to the opposite side of her skull."

Student 11: Yeah, it does say that.

Student 10: Where does it say that?

Student 11: *(Reading from the case study)* "Throws the brain against the opposite side of the skull — a jolt." Boo-ya.

Student 10: But she wasn't jolted, she got hit in the head.

Student 5: I know, but it is a similarity.

Focused on the language they will use, group members offer other possibilities for starting their sentence — "She got hit by a rock," "A thirteen-year-old girl had threw a rock at her face," "Her classmate threw a rock at her, hitting her in the nose" — but then return to discussing the choice of verb to indicate whether, as a result of the jolt to Ellen White's head, the brain moved or was thrown.

Student 11: Why can't we just put "which moved her brain to the opposite side"?

Student 2: Cause it threw it, okay?

Student 11: How did it throw it?

Student 10: Cause she threw her brain.

Student 2: Cause she went like this. (*makes backward head motion*)

Student 11: That's not throwing, that's just moving.

Finally, the issue is clarified. Students' resistance to a brain being thrown is not a question of verb choice but of conceptualizing brain matter itself.

Student 2: We got room in here? (*points to her head*) I thought it was just all brain.

Student 5: I don't know, but that's what it said, at least in this example.

Student 2: Like how can it move? Like is there like a little ball and it just... (*flips her hand back and forth rapidly, while the group laughs*) No, you know what I'm sayin,' like it's supposed to be like all there, like the skull would just

Student 11: The skull is under the skin, under the, this part.

Student 2: The brain is under the skull, yes, but like how can it throw it? Like is there any room in there?

Student 11: There's probably that, all that Jell-o stuff.

Student 10: Like all that gray matter that she said that we have.

(Crescenzi and Walqui, 2008)

Throughout this exchange, students challenge each other, but in a collegial way, exploring their understanding of brain volume and, finally, retrieving the academic language "gray matter" to replace "all that Jell-o stuff."

Once all the expert groups finish and have their answers approved by Crescenzi, they go back to their base groups to share the notes they prepared. Students are then supposed to dictate their answers to each other, clarifying points as they go, so that at the end of the process, everybody will have a fully completed matrix. Crescenzi has learned to predict that many times, rather than dictate sentences and spell new words so their peers can write them, students simply will put their notes down on the table for group members to copy. So she makes a point to explain that the dictation is necessary; it provides all students with the opportunity to practice academic language, or "psychological English," as in the following scene.

> *Two of the three recording students in this group have just finished taking dictation of the answer to question two.*
>
> Student 12: What was the third question?
>
> Student 13: Hold on, we got to let her catch up.
>
> Student 2: I'm only on number two.
>
> *(The teacher joins the group and notices that Student 13 has given Student 2 his paper to copy.)*
>
> Teacher: Ah, ah, ah, no.
>
> Student 13: No? I have to read it to her?
>
> Teacher: Yes.
>
> Student 13: Aww.
>
> Student 2: But the spelling is difficult.
>
> Teacher: He can read it and he can spell things. And he's very good at this.
>
> Student 2: Why can't I just copy it?
>
> Teacher: It doesn't help you practice the language. Doesn't help him practice the language. I want you to be able to use these academic terms.
>
> Student 2: But I know English.
>
> Teacher: Yes, but *psychological* English.

(Crescenzi and Walqui, 2008)

The end of class approaches as students complete their note taking in the matrix. By this time, most students can articulate — at least for that reading on which they became experts — more complex, interconnected ideas than they knew at the beginning of class. For example, in an after-class interview, Student 2 in the dialogue above, a second-generation English language learner who lagged behind her base group members in taking dictation, talked with Walqui about what she had learned.

> Student 2: It was really cool. This guy Phineas Gage, a long time ago, working on a construction, had an accident, a rod penetrated Phineas head. He did not die, he had frontal lobe damage, and he became angry, impatient. Before the accident he had been a nice man.
>
> AW: Why is he famous?
>
> Student 2: Because that was the first time that doctors studied why people change their personality. Sometimes it is brain damage.
>
> (Crescenzi and Walqui, 2008)

This particular student may need dictation practice, which the task affords, but the task also gives everyone in the class — English language learners and mainstream students alike — opportunities to learn disciplinary content and concepts.

Crescenzi will conclude the lesson at the next class meeting by having base groups work together to compare the four cases. Teams will also investigate a new case that they will write up.

Debriefing the first day's tasks with Walqui, Crescenzi notes that the task structures markedly increased students' engagement with the lesson materials — the same materials she had always used. Over time, task structures such as these, which keep students actively interacting with challenging content and with each other, make it possible for students to reach increasingly high-level academic goals.

It seems obvious that when offered inviting opportunities to build knowledge and academic stamina, more students are likely to meet the challenge, including, especially, those for whom the challenge is harder. In Crescenzi's class, having accepted the carefully scaffolded invitation, students had the motivating experience of succeeding in becoming knowledgeable about an academic topic. In some cases they were able to more correctly conceptualize the physical brain and to appropriate the academic language to identify it as "gray matter" rather than "Jell-o stuff" and to label its various parts. In other cases, they were able to sort through the details of particular instances of brain injury to develop more-complex conceptual networks about brain structure and function. The second-generation English language learners who were enticed to read about the alarming tamping rod that penetrated Phineas Gage's skull, for example, were also able to resolve the details of his sad case into the generative understanding of how scientists recognize "the behavioral manifestations of brain damage."

A Map of QTEL Principles in Two Lessons

How do these two lessons illustrate QTEL principles? In what ways do the lessons demonstrate quality?

In the literature lesson designed by Roza Ng and in the psychology lesson designed by Stacia Crescenzi, we can see the situated application of the principles of Quality Teaching for English Learners. Each lesson is a sound example of academic rigor, high expectations, quality interactions, and a language focus, all within the structure of quality curriculum.

Academic Rigor
Both lessons address central ideas in their respective disciplines. Ng is working on issues of characterization through a piece of canonical literature. Crescenzi is leading her students through an analysis of the structure and function of the brain. In each case, students are building content area authority, working with key disciplinary concepts. In neither class are the

English language learners engaged in the repetition or memorization of atomistic facts or ideas; instead, through participation in social interaction, they are working at the edge of their ability, participating in the development of their own expertise.

Challenges using generative cognitive skills or higher-order thinking are present in both classes. In Ng's literature class, students infer from concrete instances of behavior how the two key characters feel — what Richard Wright and his mother are worried about. During Collaborative Dialogue Writing, Ng's English language learners have to synthesize what they understand about the characters to invent appropriate lines for the characters to speak. In Crescenzi's psychology class, the instance of brain damage on which a student has become expert will anchor his or her understanding as groups work to compare and contrast cases, continuing to deepen students' understanding of the structure of the brain and how it works.

Because their teachers have structured their lessons with familiar tasks, students can concern themselves less with lesson mechanics and concentrate more on the lesson content and interactions. Furthermore, because their teachers have designed lessons that refer back to previous learning and forward to new learning, students will be able to use the ideas and cognitive skills they develop with increasing confidence as they participate in future lessons.

High Expectations

Both Ng's and Crescenzi's classes are characterized by respectful relationships and the belief that everybody is expected to succeed. The tasks presented by both teachers demonstrate high expectations but, at the same time, provide students with high levels of support.

The literature class, for example, begins with an activity that all students can successfully complete (relating a personal story about facing a difficult situation) and prepares them for the next, more difficult task of understanding the characters' feelings in the literature selection they will read. Throughout the lesson, by making students responsible to their partners and groups, as well as to her, Ng demonstrates her belief in their abilities to support each other's learning. Students respond accordingly, in one case asking to work during lunchtime to improve their collaborative dialogue. The performances clearly signal the ideas, language, and skills students are acquiring. The final activity, having student teams evaluate each other's product (the Mind Mirrors), is an example of how Ng extends students' responsibility to the larger learning community, expecting them to be thoughtful and fair in giving each other feedback (and supporting them in doing so, with a rubric).

In the psychology class, we also observe a process of student apprenticeship, which begins with alerting students to personal experiences that will help them understand the reading assignment. The Jigsaw Project, designed with texts of varied length and difficulty, accommodates the range of student abilities in Crescenzi's class. The different texts provide different entry points as needed, but the task itself is the same for all students, who interact across, as well as within, homogeneous groups. The teacher minimizes evidence of differentiation, and as a consequence, no students feel stigmatized. All students are stimulated and supported, and all can push beyond their initial level of maturation, taking responsibility to help each other learn within their expert groups and, again, in their base groups. In one group, students kid each other about using "big words," like "penetrate" instead of "went through," but the pressure from the group is to use the more academic term. We also see Crescenzi support and push students who try to get away with less effort, insisting, for example, on the importance of students dictating to each other instead of simply copying notes. "It doesn't help you practice the language.... I want you to be able to use these academic terms," she explains, holding students to her expectations for them.

In a homogeneous expert group consisting of students with the least English experience, group members benefit from an interlude of talking informally together in Spanish to relate to each other and to begin to manage the task. In this exchange between two boys, it is a student, not the teacher, who communicates high expectations despite the challenge of the work.

> Student 12: *(Skimming the Phineas Gage article)* Aaanda, miiira. [Whoa, look at that.]
>
> Student 9: Estoy, buey ya. [I am, dude.]
>
> Student 12: ¿Y esta palabra? No me veo futuro en esta clase, yo. [And that word? I don't see a future for myself in this class.]
>
> Student 9: ¿Qué? [What?]
>
> Student 12: No me veo futuro en esta clase. Voy a reprobar. [I don't see a future for myself in this class. I am going to fail.]
>
> Student 9: No más hazle asira. No más el pico y la pala. [Just do it like this. Just dig in and work hard.]
>
> (Crescenzi and Walqui, 2008)

Later, Student 12, a student who might have given up on the assignment if left to himself, patiently dictates information about Phineas Gage to his heterogeneous base group, does his part to keep the group moving, and, in turn, is treated respectfully by students who in less-scaffolded learning situations might dismiss him as less capable.

Quality Interactions

The principle that is probably most distinctive for classes with English language learners is the emphasis on structures that enable all students to participate significantly in class. While both Ng and Crescenzi deliberately choose, plan, introduce, model, and monitor the tasks, the tasks themselves are structured to require all students to interact. As students participate with partners or in small groups, no script guides what they say or decide to write. Students' dialogue is sustained, focused, and leads them to clarify ideas for themselves and others, deepening their understandings as a result. It is also interesting to see how such structures as the Round-Robin and the base group reporting in the Jigsaw Project promote democratic processes and ensure that particular students do not dominate the interactions.

Language Focus

In both of these classes, the teachers explicitly develop the language of the discipline and maximize the opportunities for every individual student to use it. In addition, they consciously try to "amplify, not simplify" their language. Knowing that, in many cases, teachers serve as the best examples of English that students have, Ng and Crescenzi purposefully model academic language. Even if students are initially surprised by the academic language they hear, they eventually get used to it and begin to appropriate it. In turn, students are encouraged to ask questions and clarify ideas that are essential for working through a text.

In both classes, the teacher signals what is essential to understand, through the use of focus questions or graphic organizers, such as the Double-Entry Journal and the Jigsaw Matrix, or in conversation. In the example below, Crescenzi helps the Phineas Gage expert group attend to the reason *psychologists* love the man who survived the penetration of a 44-inch rod through his jaw and out the top of his head.

> Teacher: Why is Phineas famous?
>
> Student 12:   Because
>
> Student 9:   Like his attitude changed, like radically.

Student 14:	He survived.
Student 9:	Yeah, that's one thing. But, like, the way he used to be, like, the way he, like, he used to be, which is his personality changed like towards people. He would get, like, mad really easy, like, and act childish not like he used to be before.
Teacher:	Okay, so he had these severe behavioral changes, and that's true, but are these changes what made him famous?

Students talk about the dramatic nature of Gage's injury and the fact that he survived, but the teacher then refocuses them on the disciplinary concept at hand.

Teacher:	Okay. So why's he famous? He had these changes, he lived, but why do psychologists love him? Why do we think he's so amazing?
Student 9:	(*Pointing to the text*) Ah, it says the quotation right here, "It was the historical beginning of the study of the biological basis of behavior."
Teacher:	Germán's got it exactly right...he changed dramatically, and that was the first that we, as psychologists or doctors, figured out that the brain controls behavior.

(Crescenzi and Walqui, 2008)

By her use of academic language, her collegial tone, and the inclusion of her students in the world of "we psychologists," Crescenzi communicates her students' promise as language learners and disciplinary thinkers.

Quality Curriculum

The lesson plans developed by Ng and Crescenzi showcase many of the task structures that QTEL advocates integrating into curriculum for English language learners. Notably, the tasks have been combined in ways that allow them to build on each other, accomplishing important academic goals, as well as specific lesson objectives. Ng's lesson demonstrates how significantly her students can be moved in their willingness to try out new language and, consequently, to construct new ideas. In Crescenzi's lesson, by combining tasks to engage her students at all levels of linguistic ability, she provides the kind of high-challenge and high-support learning experiences that can affect all students with a sense of their academic potential.

Conclusion

In this chapter we have seen two detailed lessons built upon the principles of Quality Teaching for English Learners. From the lesson plans to the transcripts of student and teacher talk, we have been able to experience real classrooms where teachers, as well as students, are creating their own expertise. These lessons, designed by teachers apprenticing QTEL practices and approaches, with their particular students in mind, demonstrate that

- a coherent theoretical foundation is in place;

- pedagogical structures, or tasks, scaffold teacher practice as well as student learning; and

- student learning creates its own momentum.

In the next chapter, we extend the discussion of curriculum, looking at the design of lessons and units of study in more detail.

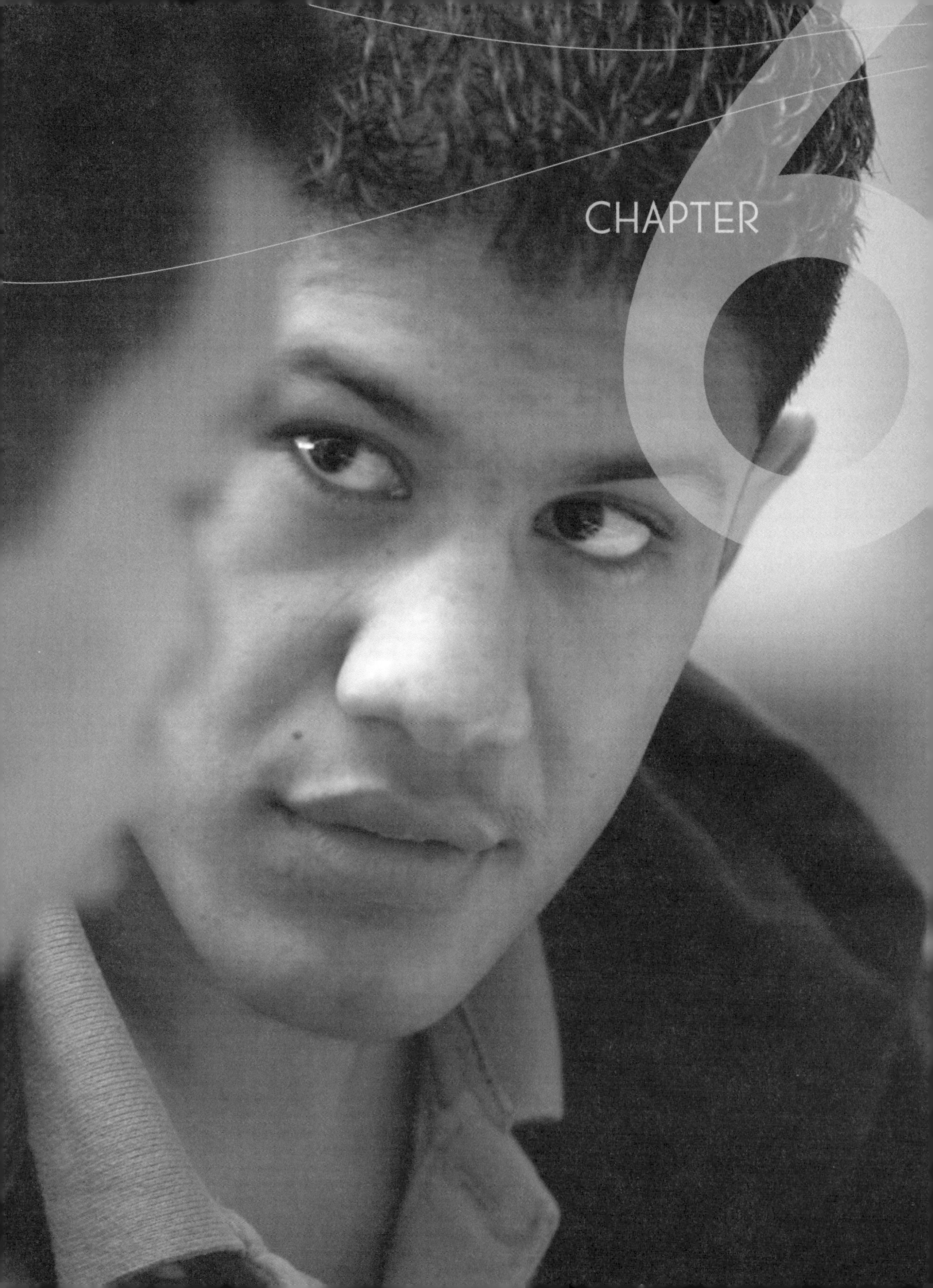

CHAPTER 6

DESIGNING INSTRUCTION

The thoughtful design of powerful, inviting, challenging, and supportive lessons is at the heart of successful learning experiences for English language learners — and all other learners as well. The "construction zone" in which such lessons are designed can be described as the space between students' understanding of a specific theme, control of a set of skills, or level of language proficiency and the objectives for a lesson, unit, and course. In this chapter we address the design of units and lessons for classes with English language learners and provide guidelines for the creation of powerful lessons.

The Need for an Inviting and Future-Oriented Pedagogy

American adolescents often complain that their education experience is unenticing, that teachers do not expect much of them, and, even, that it is difficult to stay awake in class. Visits to many classes suggest that English language learners feel this even more intensely. For these learners in particular, classroom texts frequently are of such poor quality that not even the teacher, let alone the students, can pretend to be interested. In addition to the poverty of the texts, students suffer through lessons that may consist of filling in tedious worksheets with disconnected facts. Most of the time, students may find themselves working individually and in silence. The teacher's role may seem to have been reduced to that of office manager.

Yet, in spite of this reality, students, including English learners, understand that a teacher's job is to teach — to choose instructional approaches and materials that respect learners, to create a welcoming learning environment, and to show up prepared every day. Students are acutely aware of whether teachers prepare for their job by carefully planning their lessons or not. As one student told an experienced teacher we know, months into the teacher's first year in the classroom, "We've got your number." At first, the expression was incomprehensible to the teacher, who, herself, spoke English as a second language. She thought, perhaps, that students had her phone number. But when she inquired, students clarified what they meant: "We know you well, we know how you feel about us, and we know that you care. We can tell by the effort you make, by your classes." She has always remembered that message from her students: teachers sometimes fool themselves that they are doing what is reasonably expected of them, but their students are in a position to be more critical (see, for example, Gándara and Contreras, 2009).

These students' understanding of good teaching echoes in comments made many years later by English language learners in a Los Angeles high school leadership class. Their teacher asked them to express their opinions about what makes a highly qualified teacher, knowing that, through their lived classroom experiences, these students would have much to say about teaching and were uniquely positioned to give the field useful advice (García, Agbemakplido, Abdella, Lopez, and Registe, 2006). Hanan Abdella, a senior in the class, wrote to one of his teachers, comparing his experience of her class with what he envisioned would happen in an ideal class:

> Students need to be engaged. In the first scene [your class], three students got kicked out because they were not engaged. I think it was because the lesson plan was boring. In scene two [Abdella's ideal class], the teacher knew what she was doing and had everything organized. So the students were engaged in the lesson. They were answering and asking questions, doing their work, writing in their journal....
>
> Kids learn by talking, which changes the role of being a student to that of being co-learners and co-teachers. In scene one you tell us what to write and what to think. There is no student voice in the class at all....
>
> In scene one, you were not well prepared for class. We do the same lesson plan every day, nothing new. In my ideal class, we would do different things every day to help us...discussing independent reading with the teacher and other students, and engaging in writing assignments and projects. When you are prepared for class, it shows us you took time to think through what you wanted us to learn before giving us an assignment. We know that you are ready to teach and know what you are doing when you come into the classroom." (p. 710)

Teachers' expertise manifests itself in the design and enactment of instruction that, in accordance with ambitious curricular standards, addresses the disciplinary, cognitive, and linguistic needs of students. As discussed earlier, good teaching in any context, while responding to universal principles of quality, needs to be situated in the particular — it must respond to the characteristics and needs of the particular students the teacher teaches. Good teaching is forward-looking and, instead of lamenting what the students do not have, seeks to build students' ability to reach the ambitious goals the teacher and the curriculum envision for them. Learning is made possible through a careful balance of challenge and support, a balance that helps students appropriate learning processes so that they can become increasingly autonomous learners and use these processes in their own future learning.

Such future-oriented instruction provides the structure that supports the development of students' multiple potentials. It is proleptic (see chapter 2), built with the firm belief that students will be able to become the young people they are not yet: academic thinkers, accomplished users of English across a wide variety of contexts (especially in the disciplinary fields they study), writers who communicate ideas clearly, readers who read with intellectual stamina (even materials that are not intrinsically motivating for them), and critical and discerning citizens with important choices to make.

In this chapter, we discuss several steps that effective teachers take as they plan units of study and individual lessons that challenge and support their students.

Planning Units of Study

High school and middle school teachers are rarely called on to develop an entire course. It is not uncommon, however, for teachers to develop smaller units of study, either "replacement" units intended to improve on a standard textbook treatment of a topic or units designed for specific students, including those who are English language learners. In this section, we consider the steps in planning a unit and then move on to lesson design in the subsequent section.

Determining Macro Unit Objectives

Each course in the academic curriculum has a role in the development of student expertise and states clear expectations about what the students will know and how they will be able to demonstrate this knowledge by the time they finish the course. These are the course goals. Courses are typically subdivided into units, each of which, in turn, is intended to lead to the accomplishment of a set of objectives — stages on the road to the course goals. Unit objectives specify the building blocks in that development and may be referred to as macro objectives. We can observe an example of macro unit objectives in a five-week linguistics unit that teacher Tony DeFazio designed for a high school humanities course in which students' proficiency in English ranges from beginning to intermediate levels. (See the appendix for DeFazio's description of the unit.)

Although linguistics is not necessarily a subject that would appeal to most high school students, for English language learners it is extremely relevant. As they learn English, these students can't help noticing at times how differently things are said in English from how they are said in their own language; they become aware that, in the eyes of some, certain languages appear to have more value than others; they recognize patterns in the problems they may have pronouncing particular words or intoning certain phrases. Exploring these linguistic issues is a compelling trajectory along which to develop students' academic uses of English.

DeFazio's macro objectives for his linguistics unit fall into three categories: disciplinary knowledge, generative cognitive skills, and language (see figure 15). In terms of disciplinary knowledge, DeFazio plans ways to engage students in an in-depth exploration of language, its components, and its functions in social life. Regarding generative cognitive skills, DeFazio's students will have many opportunities to define, describe, compare, contrast, analyze, and conclude. To promote students' language development,

DeFazio knows his linguistics unit will need to engage students in reading, discussing, writing, and revising a variety of texts.

Figure 15. Macro Objectives (Linguistics Unit)

Disciplinary Knowledge

Explore the topic of language in depth — its components and its functions in social life

Cognitive Skills

Use the mental operations of defining, describing, comparing, contrasting, analyzing, and concluding

Language

Use English intelligently and with increasing levels of comfort to read, discuss, write, and revise a variety of texts on language

Determining the Assessment of Macro Objectives

In concert with determining macro objectives, teachers determine what particular final assessment will allow them to evaluate whether students have accomplished the macro objectives.

DeFazio's assessment of his unit's macro objectives takes the form of a final performance, a written product that students build toward over the five weeks of the unit. A description of this product follows, with benchmark moments leading up to it.

Determining Meso Objectives, Content Topics, and Benchmark Moments

At the next level of planning, teachers determine the unit meso objectives and the related content topics. When these are set, benchmark moments are established for evaluating whether the content is providing access to and students are accomplishing the meso objectives.

For example, DeFazio has designed each week in the linguistics unit to unpack particular aspects of language, and each week students write a benchmark letter to consolidate and demonstrate the knowledge and skills they have developed so far. If we look at DeFazio's meso objectives (figure 16) for his macro *disciplinary* objective (in this case, "Explore the topic of language in depth — its components and its functions in social life"), we can anticipate the content topics that he will present to students. In figure 17, we see that DeFazio devotes one week to each topic, and he evaluates students' learning of each topic with a benchmark that he has determined to be an explanatory letter.

Figure 16. Meso Objectives for Disciplinary Macro Objective (Linguistics Unit)

Disciplinary Macro Objective

Explore the topic of language in depth — its components and its functions in social life

Disciplinary Meso Objectives

Define what is and is not a language

Understand how we learn our first and second languages

Know how many languages there are

Know whether some languages are better than others

Figure 17. Content Topics and Benchmark Moments (Linguistics Unit)

Week 1	Week 2	Week 3	Week 4	Week 5
Introduction: A System of Systems	Syntactic System in Languages	Sound System in Languages	Semantic System in Languages	Variation in Languages: Dialects, etc.
Explanatory Letter 1	Explanatory Letter 2	Explanatory Letter 3	Explanatory Letter 4	Explanatory Letter 5

A Sample Final Unit Assessment

In the linguistics unit, the final assessment is an edited collection of the five letters a student has written, explaining to someone the student knows what he or she has learned about specific aspects of language. In this unit, DeFazio determines the final assessment, or performance (the collection of letters), in conjunction with the benchmark moments (the individual letters). The benchmark moments need to signal students' readiness to execute the final performance, but the final performance needs to reflect the learning experiences that have been designed for students.

DeFazio's students write about what they find fascinating about language: "I don't know if you have heard about the kangaroo rat that stamps its feet to communicate with other rats." They report what they find unbelievable: "There are about 6800 languages in the world. Many of them are dying as I write this letter." And they offer a perspective on their own learning. Ángela, for example, who went on to graduate summa cum laude from City College of New York, wrote this advice: "Yesterday we spoke what we had learned over this research we find out that the language that is more spoken in the entire world is Chinese. The second language is English and the third is Spanish. So we need to be proud that we speak two languages."

Any teacher reading the students' letters would appreciate the depth of knowledge students have acquired about language and would be impressed by the command of language that has been developed by this focused engagement in worthy activities and ideas. The commentary that follows, by Stanford educator Kenji Hakuta, reviewing one student's set of letters from this class, is an appreciation not only of what high school English language learners can achieve, but also of what the deliberate design of powerful, inviting, challenging, and supportive instruction can inspire:

The letter format is appealing because it enables the student to readily weave between informal and formal levels of writing. Witness: "Hey grandpa, do you remember the question that I used to ask you when I was a little naughty and curious kid?" vs. "Syntax, or grammar, is the branch of linguistics dealing with the form and structure of words, and their interrelation within sentences." He even manages to use :) at the end of his letter to Jackie. This is nice because the students can appreciate the differences between formal and informal language, a phenomenon that sociolinguists call "style shifting."

The content of the letters is amazingly well developed. Even Stanford students would be challenged by this topic, yet here is an English learner beautifully writing about tree structures, rules, prescriptive grammar, and the nature of humanity! This is clear testimony to the conceptual grounding on the topic provided by Mr. DeFazio through pre-writing activities, discussions, and conceptual maps.

(personal communication, February 2009)

The Interrelationship of Disciplinary, Cognitive, and Language Objectives

As noted in the discussion of macro objectives, three categories of objectives are salient:

- *Disciplinary objectives* address the key topics, and the typical interrelationships these topics enter into in the discipline that we want students to acquire. In the case of DeFazio's linguistics unit, these objectives include understanding the nature of language, its systems, its variation, and how the ability to use language is acquired.

- *Generative cognitive objectives* are those related to academic skills such as synthesizing, explaining, comparing and contrasting, questioning, hypothesizing, and problematizing, that is, challenging the intent and value of central ideas (see chapter 4). These are the mental operations we want students to engage in as they work through the concepts and topics of focus.

- *Language objectives* relate to the language needed to be able to think, speak, write, and read about these important disciplinary concepts and topics.

It is worth discussing here what it means to maintain a deliberate focus on language. How can teachers direct students' attention at specific times to the kind of language that English language learners need to practice and, eventually, control in order to talk, read, and write about the specified academic content? Are teachers themselves aware of what exactly this language is? Of course, teachers know English well, and the more subject matter knowledge they have, the more they master the related academic English. For the most part, however, this mastery is implicit. It is almost like the air they breathe, invisible. As discussed in chapter 3, to help students focus on the language they will need to practice and use, teachers, themselves, need an awareness of the language so that they can model it appropriately and explain it when needed. While students need formal explanations of language once in a while, in subject matter classes they mostly need formulaic expressions that model and provide beginnings, transitions, and ways of ending (Ellis, 2005, 2008), as well as models of what is typically said or written by competent native speakers (e.g., the use of nominalizations, as discussed in chapter 3). They need to be provided with examples and tasks that gradually allow them to appropriate these academic uses of language (Gibbons, 2009; Schleppegrell, in press).

A teacher may find it helpful to think about language, disciplinary, and cognitive objectives separately, but these objectives mesh seamlessly as effectively designed units and lessons unfold. Consider, for example, what one of DeFazio's students wrote for a final performance: "Contrary to what many people think, there are no superior languages or language varieties. Each form is good if it meets the communication needs of people using them [sic], and if it is acceptable by their social group." From just these two sentences, we can say that this letter reflects the student's understanding of key disciplinary concepts, synthesizes this understanding in a demonstration of high-level mental operations, and uses the academic language of linguistics with sophistication. One slip notwithstanding, the letter also demonstrates technically polished English.

Planning Lessons

Lessons, as components of units, are developed with micro objectives and serve as stepping stones toward students' attainment of a unit's key concepts and skills. Lessons invite students to "play" with these concepts by engaging in the typical academic activities of those who practice the discipline: the critical review of texts; application of ideas; construction of explanations; drawing of inferences and conclusions; comparing and contrasting ideas or processes; connecting events, motivation, and action; and evaluating concepts and processes — all through oral and written discourse.

Such lessons are based on teachers' knowledge of standards, objectives, their students, what students seem to gravitate toward (sometimes to build on that inclination, sometimes to counterbalance it with other important ideas and skills students may avoid), and what students need in order to develop increasingly complex abilities. Within the parameters of a unit of study, determining students' multiple needs and deciding which multiple overlapping zones of proximal development the lesson will target establishes the basis for the lesson plan. After developing the plan, of course, next steps include getting the resources needed to carry out the lesson and engaging students in productive activity.

In the first lesson of Tony DeFazio's linguistics unit, he wants all students to uncover what they "know" about language — whether this knowledge is correct or incorrect. Students brainstorm everything they can think of, and when their ideas stall, DeFazio prompts them with questions. Once the class has brought to the surface many ideas and questions, students, regardless of their level of proficiency in English, engage in some quick research to check their ideas and explore their questions. DeFazio has gathered a wide range of resources — a wheeled library cart full of books and magazines about language. Many of these materials are in English, but some are in Spanish, Russian, Polish, Romanian, Chinese, Japanese, and other languages. Some of the texts are high school material, some are richly illustrated books for children, others are specialized publications and journals. And alongside these commercially published materials are books that were created as final performances by students in DeFazio's prior linguistics classes. This wide variety of materials provides students at all levels of academic and English proficiency with access to the same challenging research task.

An overview of the first week of DeFazio's linguistics unit (see figure 18) finds students working individually, in dyads, or in larger groups. What

Figure 18. Micro Objectives and Student Interactions (Linguistics Unit)

Week 1				
Day 1	Day 2	Day 3	Day 4	Day 5
Students brainstorm what they know about language and explore a variety of resources to begin answering introductory questions about language.	Table groups share notes, support findings, and construct semantic maps with pooled knowledge.	Students begin first letter, incorporating teacher and peer editing; they transfer initial writing to poster paper and share with the class.	Students continue research and writing, sharing their findings, and editing.	Students complete letters, addressing key questions clearly and drawing on personal examples and resources; letters are shared.

each student or dyad learns is shared with larger groups and, eventually, the whole class. In these interactions, students provide each other with learning opportunities and reasons for using and appropriating complex language. Each lesson is designed with its own micro objectives while also helping students work toward the unit's macro and meso objectives.

Continuing deeper into the design of individual lessons, we will shift from DeFazio's linguistics unit to a variety of classrooms, where we will investigate the "three moments" in a lesson and the selection of tasks that are suitable within these three moments.

Three Moments in a Lesson

A well-scaffolded lesson can be conceptualized in three moments: first, preparing learners for the learning embodied in the lesson text; second, scaffolding students' interaction with the text; and, third, extending their understanding of the ideas in the text. Figure 19 outlines the particular instructional purposes inherent in each of these moments.

In following sections of this chapter, we will look at examples of the kinds of tasks that help learners achieve the purposes of each moment in a lesson.

Within each moment, activity structures we call tasks are designed to address the varying purposes in a lesson moment. As defined earlier, all tasks are activities in which students use language to share, or compare, with each other the ideas and information that the different participants have. So, for example, tasks present students with ways to explore "gaps" of experience, information, and opinion. Tasks *require* dialogue and collaboration.

Another defining characteristic of tasks is their focus on developing meaning — within the well-known structure of the task itself — that facilitates student participation even when lesson concepts and language are beyond

Figure 19. Purposes Related to the Three Moments in a Lesson

1. Preparing Learners	· Focus attention on concepts to be developed · Activate (or build) relevant background knowledge · Introduce essential vocabulary in context
2. Interacting with Text	· Deconstruct text; focus on understanding a chunk · Reconnect chunk to whole text · Establish connections between ideas within text
3. Extending Understanding	· Re-create text in a new genre or create new text based on new understanding · Apply newly gained knowledge to novel situations or use to problem-solve · Connect ideas learned to other ideas outside the text

students' competence. Tasks are the scaffolding *structures* that foster students' optimal learning during each of three lesson moments.

If we return to Roza Ng's lesson plan for the "Hunger" excerpt from Richard Wright's biography, *Black Boy,* we can easily identify how the tasks in her lesson support her purposes for each moment of the lesson (see figure 20). She uses Think-Pair-Share and Class Round-Robin in the *Preparing Learners* moment; she uses Partner Reading, the Double-Entry Journal, and Partner Sharing in the *Interacting with Text* moment; and she uses Collaborative Dialogue, Mind Mirror, and Gallery Walk in the *Extending Understanding* moment.

1. Preparing Learners

All lessons for English language learners begin by getting students ready to make sense of the lesson ahead. The Preparing Learners part of a lesson has three main purposes:

Figure 20. Task Selection Examples for Three Moments of the "Hunger" Lesson

Lesson Objectives: Students will learn about characterization in literature, tracing the development of characters over time and providing evidence for their conclusions.	
Preparing Learners	
Think-Pair-Share	Partners tell each other about a time when they faced a difficult situation.
Class Round-Robin	Students relate their partner's and their own difficult situations to the class.
Interacting with Text	
Partner Reading and Discussion	Partners each read the text about a difficult situation, one focusing on one of the main characters and the other partner focusing on the other character. They then discuss their characters' actions and emotions.
Teacher Model	The teacher models how to record observations and evidence in the Double-Entry Journal.
Double-Entry Journal	In expert groups of four assigned to focus on one of the two main characters, students individually reread the text and make journal notes about how the character is feeling, with textual evidence to support their observations. Group members share their notes and reach agreement about their ideas and evidence.
Partner Sharing	Group members return to their original partners and exchange information about their characters.
Extending Understanding	
Individual Reading	Students silently reread the text.
Collaborative Dialogue Writing	Groups of four write an extended dialogue to illuminate a particular move in the story. They practice dramatic readings of their script.
Dialogue Performance	Groups perform for their classmates.
Reflection on the Double-Entry Journal	Students each review and add to or revise their journal notes based on what they learned from classmates' performances.
Mind Mirror	Groups of four create a poster that conveys in quotations, original phrases, symbols, and drawings a main character's state of mind at one point in the story.
Mind Mirror Rubric	Using a rubric, groups rate their poster and write an explanation of their rating.
Gallery Walk	Groups review the other posters created for the same character they featured. They use the rubric to write their evaluations.

- to establish an interest in and focus for the lesson,

- to activate students' relevant prior knowledge connected to the theme and relationships identified by the lesson objective, and

- to introduce a few of the most essential new words, in context.

During any school day, middle and high school students carry with them a number of preoccupations from their home, neighborhood, and relationships with friends. Additionally, as they continuously move from class to class, they are affected by a wide variety of stimuli, some pleasant, some not so. These preoccupations and distractions compete with adolescents' engagement in schoolwork. If we want them to profitably participate in our lessons, we need to be ready to refocus and re-engage them every time they walk into class. This is impossible to do without well-scaffolded lessons.

A well-scaffolded lesson for adolescents entices them to participate in activities that focus on key disciplinary topics and skills but, also, that address students' emerging identity, help them establish new and more mature relations with peers of both sexes, and engage them in an examination of the variety of information and roles that need to be considered in order to make informed choices. Accomplishing these objectives with native speakers of English is important enough; with English language learners, being sensitive to students' identities, as well as to their academic needs, is perhaps even more important. Second language learners who are first generation in the United States not only have to deal with lessons in a language they do not speak, but also have to do so in a completely new environment. When English language learners are second or third generation in this country, their very status as nonproficient English speakers suggests that they exist within contexts that have not valued or supported them in the past.

Readying adolescent English learners for the lesson ahead by demonstrating the personal relevance topics have for them and engaging them in deliberate activity that promotes solidarity with peers is essential. In addition, the more we help students activate their prior experiences and create their own learning goals before the substance of the lesson is unpacked, the more benefit they will be able to derive from it.

Teachers gain as well from inviting their students to engage in Preparing Learners activities. At times they will be able to observe what students gravitate toward, getting to know them better in order to use this knowledge for future lessons. At other times they will gain appreciation for the funds of knowledge students bring to school, gaining insight into the families and communities their students represent. Oftentimes, teachers will learn about misconceptions students have and thus can prepare better for the cognitive dissonance the lesson will generate.

Figure 21 identifies sample tasks for the purpose of Preparing Learners, tasks that are described in more detail following the figure.

Figure 21. Examples of Tasks for Preparing Learners

Preparing Learners	Sample Tasks in Chapter 6
Focus attention on concepts to be developed	Think-Pair-Share Quick-Write/Round-Robin Anticipatory Guide or Extended Anticipatory Guide
Activate (or build) relevant background knowledge	Think-Pair-Share Quick-Write/Round-Robin Novel Ideas Only Jigsaw Project
Introduce vocabulary in context	Anticipatory Guide or Extended Anticipatory Guide

Think-Pair-Share. In the prior chapter, Roza Ng started her class with a Think-Pair-Share task designed to focus students on a time they faced a difficult situation, a concept that would be developed in the text they were about to read. Think-Pair-Share is an extremely flexible task, and regardless of the text to be read or prior knowledge to be activated, the task has a predictable, easy-to-learn organization:

- Students work in dyads.

- The teacher asks students to think about a scenario or a couple of questions (writing the prompt for all to see).

- Students have one or two minutes to individually jot down ideas.

- Students start working in dyadic interaction: Student 1 asks Student 2 the questions or prompt.

- Student 2 responds and, after the response, presents the same questions or prompts to Student 1.

- Student 1 responds.

- When called upon by the teacher to share information, chosen students share first their partner's answer and then their own.

Among the students' stories about facing a difficult situation and how the incident made them feel were some that were almost universal for these English language learners (e.g., embarrassment in having to take a test in English days after arriving in their new country, distress in trying to ask permission to go to the bathroom, humiliation in writing an essay without enough English to complete a thought) and others that were less common, but equally revealing (e.g., being bullied in a prior school or robbed of the subway fare to get home). As students shared these experiences, they had an opportunity to examine themselves and their classmates in a wide variety of situations and roles, project their evolving identities, and empathize with each other. As preparation for their future interaction with the lesson text, the task alerted students to experiences that would make it easier for them to read about, understand, and empathize with Richard Wright's traumatic childhood experience.

Quick-Write/Round-Robin. In Stacia Crescenzi's class, also in chapter 5, we saw a similar Preparing Learners task — a Quick-Write followed by a Round-Robin. As with the Think-Pair-Share, the purpose was to focus students on concepts that would be developed in the text and to activate their relevant prior knowledge, in this case about someone who had had an accident and its effect on the person. Students were organized in groups of four, and their teacher asked them to write in complete sentences (consonant with one of her course goals, to improve students' writing skills) that they would then take turns reading to their fellow group members.

The Quick-Write/Round-Robin task has a predictable organization:

- Students work in groups of four.
- The teacher asks students to think about a scenario or a couple of questions (writing the prompt for all to see).
- Students have two or three minutes to individually write down their answers.
- Students take turns reading what they have written to the group. Group members do not interrupt or comment.
- When all students have had a turn reading their narrative to the group, group members may ask each other questions, comment, compare ideas, and otherwise discuss what group members' narratives reveal.
- When groups have completed their discussions, the teacher may call on students to relate a story from their group or to report on their group's discussion.

Because the students in Crescenzi's class were studying brain structure and function, the purpose of the task was to alert them to the different ways that brain injuries may affect people. As with the Think-Pair-Share in Ng's class, students were engaged, sharing personal experiences, and moving into important academic explorations. Furthermore, participation in the tasks had additional advantages:

- Students begin by quietly writing down some ideas. As students write, the teacher circulates, noting students' responses and helping those who have not written anything or have misunderstood the prompt.

- The tasks get students talking and using language that is beyond their current competence, especially the language that is modeled in the question.

- The tasks focus students on meaning, on the experiences they are relating and learning about, and it allows for the emergence of novelty.

- The tasks place each student in a position of authority, able to pro-actively use his or her assets (and liabilities).

- All students have the opportunity to talk, listen, and understand; those who report to the class practice paraphrasing what they learn from others as well.

Each task has the purpose of moving students one step closer to the lesson objectives. Consequently, each task should support students in precise ways. The Think-Pair-Share and the Quick-Write/Round-Robin tasks create a bridge to students' experiences and give them the opportunity to construct schema as they connect the diverse narratives they hear their classmates share. A positive and respectful classroom climate is a *sine qua non* for the productive integration of the cognitive, social, and emotional skills that these tasks foster. The questions or prompts that drive either task must be deliberately crafted to elicit experiences, emotions, or ideas that will help students navigate the lesson or text at hand.

Novel Ideas Only. This particular Preparing Learners task is a quick way to elicit the knowledge or intuitions that reside in a whole class about a specific topic, alerting students to check for these and related ideas as they then interact with the topic in a new text.

Novel Ideas Only has a predictable organization:

- Students begin work in groups of four.

- The teacher asks students to think about a topic or question.

- Students each write the prompt and number their paper for a list.

- Students have one minute to individually brainstorm and write down their ideas.

- Student A reads from his or her paper one idea to the group.

- Student B echoes the idea and group members add it to their lists.

- Student B reads from his or her paper one idea (that is different from the idea already given) to the group.

- Student C echoes the idea and group members add it to their lists.

- Student C reads from his or her paper one idea (that is different from the ideas already given) to the group.

- Student D echoes the idea, and so forth.

- After all novel ideas within a group have been given and written on the group members' lists, students draw a line under the last item on their lists.

- The teacher calls on one member of a group to read the group's list of ideas.

- All other groups monitor their own lists, adding (below the line they have drawn) any ideas that are novel and checking off any of their ideas (above the line) that have been given.

- The teacher calls on one member of another group, who then reads to the class any remaining novel ideas on that group's above-the-line list.

- The teacher calls on groups until all novel ideas have been given.

For example, students in a high school class who are about to read Guy de Maupassant's short story "The Necklace" hypothesize what a story so titled may be about, calling on their prior knowledge of necklaces, human nature, and the structure of short stories. In the extract below, one group is beginning to build their group list:

Student 1: I think a story titled "The Necklace" may be about...a beautiful necklace.

Student 2: Student 1 thinks a story titled "The Necklace" may be about a beautiful necklace. I think it may be about people who like necklaces.

Student 3: Student 2 thinks a story titled "The Necklace" may be about people who like necklaces. I think a story titled "The Necklace" may be about someone who loses a necklace.

Student 4: Student 3 thinks the story may be about someone who loses a necklace. I think it may be about a necklace that represents something. *(points proprietarily to her own necklace)*

(Ryan and Walqui, 2008)

When groups then share their ideas with the class, students react to their classmates' ideas, and interest in the story possibilities builds. By the time all the ideas are reported, everyone in the class has heard a range of novel ideas, including that the story will be about "rich peoples' lives," "someone obsessed with a necklace," "a necklace that was stolen," and "a mom passing a necklace on to her daughter." Students engage with Guy de Maupassant's story prepared to check what they and classmates have predicted and to entertain what will turn out to be yet another novel idea — the author's.

Jigsaw Project. Sometimes personal experience or prediction is not the right place to start a lesson. For example, if English language learners are going to read *Macbeth* in a high school language arts class, preparing them for the experience will require building some background knowledge.

The Jigsaw Project has a predictable organization:

- The teacher prepares a set of related texts, only one of which will be read by any individual student.

- Students are assigned to "base" groups of four.

- One student from each base group joins one of four "expert" groups.

- Expert groups each read a different assigned text and collaborate on answering a set of questions (each expert group has the same set of questions).

- The teacher reviews and approves groups' answers.

- Expert group members all copy the approved answers and return to their original base groups.

- Base group members share information from their expert groups and compare and contrast what each has learned.

In the example shown in figure 22, from a QTEL-designed *Macbeth* unit (2006), the Jigsaw Project task is devised to help students situate themselves in Elizabethan England. Students each gain expertise in a specific element of Elizabethan life: the man called Shakespeare, the theater during his times, the English spoken at the time, and the relevance of his work. Students read brief articles written specifically to present linguistic abundance — amplified rather than simplified (i.e., stripped down and decontextualized).

Figure 22. Jigsaw Matrix: Shakespeare and His Times

	Elizabethan Theater	Shakespeare's Life	Shakespeare's Language	Shakespeare's Relevance
What are some of the main points the article makes? What did you learn that you found interesting?				
How are things similar and different today?				
What else would you like to find out about the topic? Write down two or three questions.				

After reading individually, students discuss the Jigsaw Matrix questions, write consensus answers for the teacher to review, and then write the approved answers to report back to their base groups. (Review by the teacher is an important step to eliminate the risk that students may adopt or transmit incorrect ideas or language.) When students rejoin their original groups, they share and dictate or explain their answers (depending on their level of English competence) while their peers take notes. This task may take most of a 55-minute class, but it will have prepared students to take the next step in a unit focused on Shakespeare's tragedy.

During the *Preparing Learners* moment of a lesson, a single task may not provide enough support for students to begin a new text. In the jigsaw above, for example, students will have gained an understanding of the Shakespearean context, but they are not yet ready to engage with the complexities of *Macbeth*; they need opportunities to focus on the core concepts developed in the play.

Anticipatory Guide. The Anticipatory Guide is designed to start students thinking about some of the key ideas that will be explored in a text. These themes are framed broadly as statements for students to evaluate before they experience and unpack them as manifested in the text.

The Anticipatory Guide has a predictable structure, but one that shifts slightly as students apprentice this task:

Initially,

- Students work in dyads.

- Together they read and consider each statement.

- Each partner explains his or her response to each statement.

With practice,

- Students work in dyads.

- Individually and silently, each responds to each statement.

- Together they compare answers orally.

- Each partner explains his or her thinking.

Eventually,

- Students internalize the value of anticipating the themes, topics, and developments that a text presents.

In the Anticipatory Guide in figure 23, five general statements (abstracted from specific themes in *Macbeth*) are presented. Some are true, some are false, and some are subject to interpretation. Each will be salient in students' understanding and interpretation of the play.

Figure 23. Anticipatory Guide: *Macbeth*

Directions: Read each of the following statements and decide whether you agree or not.		
	Agree	**Disagree**
1. Some people do not feel guilt. That is to say, they do not feel bad when they do something wrong.	X	
2. Keeping secrets can hurt you because it is not good to keep things inside.		X
3. There is no such thing as fate or destiny. In other words, we CAN control our future.		
4. Committing one crime leads to committing more crimes.		
5. Ambition is a positive trait or characteristic.		

To support the interactive nature of the activity, the teacher provides formulaic expressions for the expected exchange so that students can use them. Figure 24 is an example the teacher might provide partners working together on an Anticipatory Guide.

Figure 24. Sample Formulaic Expressions for Working on an Anticipatory Guide

Student 1:   I will read statement one. It says_____. I agree/disagree with it because _____. So, I am going to mark it agree/disagree. What do you think?

Student 2:   I agree/disagree with you because _____. So, for statement one, I will mark agree/disagree. Now let me read statement two. It says _____. I agree/...

An activity like this one enables students to use language that may be beyond their individual ability to produce while allowing them take a stand with regard to ideas that will be elaborated later. If students don't understand one of the statements, they ask for clarification from their partner, from other groups, or from the teacher. In this way, what is not known has surfaced, and what is known or believed has been expressed and recorded as evidence of beliefs.

Sometimes Anticipatory Guides include both the anticipatory reaction and the final confirmation after the lesson or unit has been completed. In the example of an Extended Anticipatory Guide in figure 25, students go back to their original responses to see whether their ideas were supported by evidence in the play.

Anticipatory Guides can be used to prepare learners for text in a variety of genres, not only fiction. For example, the Extended Anticipatory Guide in figure 26 was written for a middle school lesson focusing on biography. The teacher selected a text presenting the life of Marian Anderson.

In selecting an article about Marian Anderson, the teacher chose the biography of somebody she admires and about whom she has enough knowledge and passion to communicate easily with her students. In designing this Extended Anticipatory Guide, the teacher's purpose is to get students thinking about issues of social justice and discrimination, as well as about music and singers. The guide is also designed to introduce key vocabulary that students will need as they read the text (democracy, privilege, ancestry, discrimination, opera). The guide also serves as an informal assessment of how much students know about the lesson topics and how they feel about them, alerting the teacher to potential areas of focus before or as students interact with the text.

Figure 25. Extended Anticipatory Guide: *Macbeth*

Directions Part 1: Read each of the following statements and decide whether you agree or not.			Directions Part 2: After you have read *Macbeth*, what evidence in the play supports or does not support your response in Part 1?
	Agree	Disagree	What I found out in the text
1. Some people do not feel guilt. That is to say, they do not feel bad when they do something wrong.	X		Macbeth felt very guilty and so did his wife
2. Keeping secrets can hurt you because it is not good to keep things inside.		X	Keeping secrets hurt both Macbeth and Lady Macbeth
3. There is no such thing as fate. In other words, we CAN control our destiny.			
4. Committing one crime leads to committing more crimes.			
5. Ambition is a positive trait or characteristic.			

Figure 26. Extended Anticipatory Guide: Marian Anderson

			Directions Part 2: After you have read about Marian Anderson, what evidence in the article supports or does not support your response in Part 1?
Directions Part 1: Read each of the following statements and decide whether you agree or not.			
	Agree	Disagree	What I found out in the text
1. As a proud democracy, the United States of America has always provided all individuals with equal rights or privileges.			
2. For much of U.S. history, Africans and their descendents had to use facilities (schools, bathrooms, restaurants, etc.) that were separate from those used by other people, especially those with European ancestry.			
3. To discriminate means to treat diverse or different groups of people with equal practices and respect.			
4. Knowing multiple languages is important. Opera singers, for example, benefit from knowing several languages.			
5. Anyone with a fine voice can become a professional opera singer. Special studies may be helpful, but they are not required to perform at world-famous opera theaters such as the Metropolitan Opera House in New York City.			

2. Interacting with Text

As teachers plan activities to invite students to work through the text, they pay attention to its key constituents. Beyond being familiar with a text, teachers must consider which of its ideas are substantive and generative for their students' academic development (and which ones, although perhaps interesting or important, will be left aside); how these ideas interconnect in key relationships with each other; and, consequently, where teachers expect to scaffold students' development and construction of understanding.

Three broad purposes need to be accomplished during the *Interacting with Text* part of a lesson:

- The text is deconstructed into its constitutive focus ideas, and students explore a chunk at a time to understand its meaning and significance.

- Ideas are reconnected back to the emerging whole, and students make sense of them in the larger context of the text.

- Relationships or connections are established so that students make links between what otherwise may seem to be disparate facts and ideas in the text.

Teachers, then, need to use pedagogical x-ray vision to discern from a text the main ideas and the ways in which they are articulated to form a body of knowledge. Accordingly, teachers design activities that will alert students to these constructs and their interconnections by engaging students in social interaction. This work entails taking students beyond the surface of a text, or the identification or recall of facts, and leading them, for example, into interpretation, logical inference, explanation, hypothesis, and prediction.

As is true of the *Preparing Learners* tasks, each task in the *Interacting with Text* moment of a lesson must be purposely designed to move students toward a lesson's objectives. Figure 27 lists examples of such tasks, designed specifically to help students interact with text.

Figure 27. Examples of Tasks That Support Interacting with Text

Interacting with Text	Sample Tasks in Chapter 6
Deconstruct text; focus on understanding a chunk	Double-Entry Journal Reading with a Focus Viewing with a Focus Clarifying Bookmark or Partner Clarifying Bookmark
Reconnect a chunk to the emerging whole text	Double-Entry Journal Triple-Entry Journal Clarifying Bookmark or Partner Clarifying Bookmark
Establish connections between ideas within text	Double-Entry Journal Triple-Entry Journal Clarifying Bookmark or Partner Clarifying Bookmark

Double-Entry Journal. Also known as a dialectical journal, this is a two-column chart in which students are asked to do something in the left-hand space and to support their work with evidence in the right-hand space. In chapter 5, we saw how Roza Ng invited her students to read an excerpt from *Black Boy,* decide how a character thinks and feels, and provide evidence by using specific quotes from the text. Figure 28 illustrates how variations may be introduced. For example, any of the questions in the figure can help students carefully read through key passages of a text. Once students interact with the text, of course, they interact with each other, typically in dyads or groups of four to compare and discuss their answers.

Figure 28. Variations on a Double-Entry Journal

How does this character think? What does he or she feel?	What is your evidence? Write down specific quotes.

What does the character do? (Quote evidence from the text.)	What are possible implications of the character's actions?

What does the character do? (Paraphrase from the text.)	What would I have done in this character's place and why?

What does the character do? (Quote evidence from the text.)	What does the action signal about the character's state of mind?

During the *Macbeth* unit, one Double-Entry Journal, shown in figure 29, asks student dyads to predict what Macbeth will do next and how Banquo will react to Macbeth's actions. Dyads write their prediction in the left column and support it in the right column with quotes from the play or relevant evidence from their own experience.

Figure 29. Double-Entry Journal: Prediction at the End of *Macbeth* Act I, Scene IV

What will Macbeth do next and how will Banquo react?	What elements of the text or our own interpretation lend support to this conjecture?

Reading with a Focus. In this task, students are given two or three questions before they read a passage in the text. The focus questions alert students to what the teacher considers most important for the class to understand. For English language learners, the focus questions help them navigate the difficulties of the text without unnecessary tension. Reading with a Focus, in other words, gives English language learners a schema for the reading and permission to not understand everything.

The example in figure 30 helps students maintain a focus on what is most important for them to understand from a particular chunk of *Macbeth*.

Figure 30. Reading with a Focus: *Macbeth* Act I, Scene II

Ask students to read Act I, scene ii silently. Explain that in this scene Macbeth and his best friend, Banquo, meet the three witches, the "weird ones," who tell them what will happen in the future. Let students know that as they read the scene, all they need to understand are the answers to the following questions:

· What do the three witches predict for Macbeth (lines 49–51) and Banquo (lines 66–68)?

· How do the two friends react to these prophecies?

· Ask students to take notes to help them prepare to answer the questions.

After students have struggled with the text and have come up with answers to the questions, lead a class discussion of their answers, clarifying the prophecy. Point students' attention to the apparent contradictions in the text. How may they be explained? This is a question to be revisited at the end of the play.

Viewing with a Focus. Similar to Reading with a Focus, the Viewing with a Focus task scaffolds students' interaction with visual text — short DVD or other video clips. These clips are carefully selected to help students meet specific lesson objectives. For example, in the *Macbeth* unit, students visualize particular scenes from the play and then view the same scenes excerpted from a film production (see figure 31). Viewing with a Focus questions help students deepen their understanding of a scene by comparing their visualizations with those of the filmmaker (and the peers in their groups of four).

Figure 31. Viewing with a Focus: Encountering *Macbeth*'s Witches

What does Act I, scene iii look like in my imagination?		
How do I imagine Macbeth?	How do I imagine Banquo?	How do I imagine the witches?

What does the scene look like according to the filmmaker?		
What does Macbeth look like according to the filmmaker?	What does Banquo look like according to the filmmaker?	What do the witches look like according to the filmmaker?

Macbeth is an extremely complex piece of literature, even for high school students who are native speakers of English. For English language learners, the complexity is compounded. At the same time, they have much to gain from the effort of working through the play to understand its themes, become familiar with Shakespearean language, and build intellectual stamina. The tasks that structure their interaction with the text scaffold understanding in part by ensuring meaningful peer and teacher interactions.

Clarifying Bookmark. The Clarifying Bookmark task asks students to deliberately think about what they need to do when they encounter difficulties with a text. The bookmark provides language routines they may use to accomplish their actions. Students develop metacognitive awareness by applying specific strategies to solve their reading difficulties. Because four different strategies are presented (see figure 32), the bookmark is presented and practiced over time, one set of strategies at a time, with multiple opportunities to practice before another set is introduced.

The bookmark includes different ways of approaching each of the strategy areas and gives students choices about how to proceed; even when students are in the process of learning a new language, they appreciate opportunities to exercise a degree of autonomy. While the Clarifying Bookmark task is extremely useful and generative for students, it also requires a degree of teacher stamina to introduce its parts and ensure that students get enough practice using them so that they internalize the strategies.

Clarifying Bookmark for Partner Reading. One way to ease students into the process outlined in the Clarifying Bookmark is to begin with a bookmark designed for partner reading. This more targeted option focuses students on summarizing, with clarifying a second step if called for. Partners start from formulaic expressions to build their understandings or to articulate particular areas of confusion. As shown in figure 33, the Clarifying Bookmark for Partner Reading has the additional feature of structuring student interactions: "What *you* can say" after reading a chunk of text aloud and "What *your partner* can say" in response.

A further purpose of the Clarifying Bookmark for Partner Reading task is to scaffold students' comfort moving along the continuum of language use, from conversational to academic. Initially, students may combine the formulaic expressions with academic language in the text, repeating the words but perhaps not fully understanding the meaning. Later, students may substitute their own constructions, signaling more comfort with the language meaning. Finally, students may return to the more formal, academic language because they fully understand it, it is precise, and they know how to use it (i.e., they have appropriated it).

Figure 32. Clarifying Bookmark

What You Can Do	What You Can Say
1. Identify confusion as you go.	Did my attention wander? Is vocabulary stopping me? Are pronouns stopping me? Am I confused about a particular phrase or sentence?
2. Reread. Look for context clues.	First, I should reread the sentence where I got confused. Second, if I'm still confused, I should reread the prior sentence. Third, if I'm still confused, I should reread the sentence after the one where I got confused.
3. Make connections to background knowledge.	What do I know about this topic? Where have I seen or heard something like this before? This concept or idea is related to...
4. Make your best guess at the gist of the text chunk.	Even though I'm not sure, I think this text chunk means... A sensible meaning for this text chunk might be... This text chunk seems to be about something like...

Figure 33. Clarifying Bookmark for Partner Reading

	What You Can Say	**What Your Partner Can Say**
Summarize	"I understand this part, and I can summarize it in this way…" "I can paraphrase this part in these words…"	"I agree/disagree because…" "I agree/disagree and I would like to add…" "I think what you are confused about means…"
Clarify	"I understand that this part means…, but I am confused about…" "I have a question about… because…"	"I am confused about that part also because…" "I don't understand. Could you explain more?"

Triple-Entry Journal. The Triple-Entry Journal task helps students sort out or change complex ideas. In the first example of a Triple-entry Journal (see figure 34), from the *Macbeth* unit, we can see that one purpose of the Triple-Entry Journal is to raise or reinforce students' awareness of the power of language at different levels, including at the psychological level. In this example, students reflect on how language is used in a particular section of the play. They choose one character's lines and reflect on the ways in which this character tries to convince another to go against his or her will. (Sociolinguists might describe the three columns in the Triple-Entry Journal examples that follow as "locution" (what is said), "illocution" (what is meant by what is said), and "perlocution" (what effect it has on the listener.)

Figure 34. Triple-Entry Journal: Seeing Behind Language

What does the character say? Identify the character and copy the dialogue you will analyze.	What does the character mean? Explain what the character would say if he or she were not masking his or her intentions.	What is the character accomplishing? By saying this, what is he or she actually doing to others?

In another use of the Triple-Entry Journal task (see figure 35), students might record initial understanding or beliefs, intervening evidence, and revised or expanded understanding or beliefs. So, for example, students might track their changing understanding of the term "calorie" as they read a biology assignment. (Their initial understanding would be recorded as a Preparing Learners task.)

Figure 35. Triple-Entry Journal: How My Thinking Changed

What I think "calorie" means	What I learned about "calorie"	How my thinking changed

A more open-ended version for having students record the evolution of their thinking is the "I saw, I thought, I found out" progression. This structure encourages students to be metacognitive, to be aware of their thinking processes in the moment. For example, the student on page 27 who read the

Fourteenth Amendment might have recorded the evolution of her thinking in a Triple-Entry Journal as shown in figure 36.

Figure 36. Triple-Entry Journal: What I Noticed About My Thinking

What I read that got my attention	What it made me think about	What I think now that I found out more
No State shall make or enforce any law which shall abridge the privileges or immunities of CITIZENS of the United States; NOR shall any State deprive any PERSON…equal protection of the laws.	Undocumented immigrants are not CITIZENS, but they are PERSONS. Do you have to be a citizen or only a PERSON to be protected by U.S. laws?	The 14th Amendment says no PERSON shall be deprived of equal protection. But undocumented immigrants don't seem to have equal rights (to a speedy trial, for example). I wonder…

3. Extending Understanding

After students work deliberately through a text, with the teacher's guidance and support, they need to extend their understanding of the text, connect it to other ideas beyond the text, and apply their new learning to multiple other situations. In designing lessons, this third moment of a lesson is when teachers present students with invitations to engage in Extending Understanding tasks.

Most teachers recognize the value of culminating activities that follow students' completion of a text. A typical assignment might be for students to write an essay. However, most students benefit also from completing *Extending Understanding* tasks that take up text ideas in more playful or tightly focused ways or as stepping stones toward more complex assignments.

These tasks have the purpose of extending and deepening students' understanding in the following ways:

- Students use their understanding of the text to create and/or re-create a representation of its important ideas.

- Students apply their newly gained knowledge and skills to the solution of novel problems.

- Students connect new ideas to ideas gained through other lessons, other courses, and life experiences, putting them all in perspective.

Teachers design Extending Understanding tasks that help students reflect and consolidate learning, even as the learning is being applied in new ways and to new situations. Such tasks are also an opportunity for students to celebrate their accomplishment of lesson and unit objectives. Figure 37 highlights examples of such tasks, which are discussed in the pages that follow.

Figure 37. Examples of Tasks That Extend Understanding

Extending Understanding	Sample Tasks in Chapter 6
Re-create text in a new genre or create new text to represent new understanding	Collaborative Mind Mirror Monologue Famous Phrases
Apply newly gained knowledge to novel situations or use to problem-solve	Monologue Create, Exchange, Assess
Connect ideas learned to other ideas and experiences outside the text	Famous Phrases Collaborative Dialogue Writing Literary Elements

Collaborative Mind Mirror. The Collaborative Mind Mirror task allows groups of four students to synthesize and represent their understanding of a character in literature or history. As we saw in Roza Ng's lesson in chapter 5, students imagine their selected character looking in the mirror, but instead of seeing a physical reflection, the character sees his or her inner mind: a combination of thoughts, needs, wishes, fears, and so on. To express these ideas, students create a collaborative poster of their character's psyche.

The Collaborative Mind Mirror task has a predictable structure:

- To make criteria for the performance transparent to students, the teacher reviews a rubric outlining successful completion of the task.

- Groups select a character to represent.

- Inside a large outline of the character's head, group members write and/or illustrate at least four elements of the character's inner life:
  — two quotes from the text that reveal the essence of the character's state of mind,
  — two original phrases the team creates to show key ideas or feelings going through the character's head,
  — two symbols related to the character's condition, and
  — two drawings related to the character's state of mind.
- Group members use the rubric to rate their Mind Mirror; they state three reasons for their assessment.

In the QTEL *Macbeth* unit, for example, students create mind maps for either Macbeth or Lady Macbeth, at two points in the characters' development. Groups assess their work with the rubric shown in figure 38, building the metacognitve ability to apply criteria to their own work.

Figure 38. Collaborative Mind Mirror Rubric

Performance Indicators	Outstanding	Passing	Needs Revision
Content	· The Mind Mirror includes two or more quotations from the text that reveal the essence of the character's state of mind.	· The Mind Mirror includes two quotations from the text related to the character's thinking.	· The Mind Mirror lacks two or more of the following: — quotations — phrases — symbols — drawings
	· The Mind Mirror includes two or more original phrases that synthesize important ideas about the character's state of mind.	· The Mind Mirror includes two original phrases based on the character's thinking.	
	· The Mind Mirror includes two or more symbols that communicate relevant ideas about the character's condition.	· The Mind Mirror includes two symbols related to the character's thinking.	
	· The Mind Mirror includes two drawings that communicate the character's state of mind.	· The Mind Mirror includes two drawings related to the character's thinking.	
	· As a whole, the Mind Mirror successfully communicates important ideas about the character's situation and state of mind.	· As a whole, the Mind Mirror communicates ideas about the character's situation and state of mind.	· The Mind Mirror as a whole does not communicate the character's situation and state of mind.
Presentation	· Each member of the group contributed to the Mind Mirror and any oral presentation.	· Each member of the group contributed to the Mind Mirror and any oral presentation.	· One or more members of the group did not contribute to the Mind Mirror or any oral presentation.
	· The Mind Mirror is neat and attractive.	· The Mind Mirror is neat.	· The Mind Mirror is sloppy.
	· The Mind Mirror uses creative wording and design to persuade the viewer.		

Monologue. The Monologue task is related to the Mind Mirror in asking students to go inside a character's mind. In this task, students write a monologue that a historic figure or literary character might voice at a particular point in time or a text.

In the *Macbeth* unit, students each write a monologue for Lady Macbeth as if she suddenly woke up during her sleepwalking scene. They are prompted to address a particular set of questions: What is troubling her? What might she say now? What would she admit to?

Famous Phrases. Some texts lend themselves to the Famous Phrases task. This task has a predictable structure that moves students from individual choice to public performance:

- Students each choose five "famous" phrases from a set provided by the teacher.

- Students memorize their five phrases.

- Students rewrite their phrases in their own words and can explain why each phrase is significant.

- For each phrase, students prepare an answer to this question: Why is this phrase still relevant (or not) today?

- The teacher polls the class to see which phrase each student prefers to perform, negotiating to distribute the performances across all phrases in the set.

- Students each perform a quote from memory, restate it in their own words, explain its significance, and explain its relative relevance in current times.

Macbeth, certainly, is a text that lends itself to this task. Consider, for example, how students might work with the excerpts in figure 39 to extend their understanding of the play and connect it to their own experience.

Figure 39. A Set of Famous Phrases from *Macbeth*

1. "Fair is foul and foul is fair."
   (The three witches in Act I, scene i, line 11)

2. "So foul and fair a day I have not seen."
   (Macbeth in Act I, scene iii, line 38)

3. "Nothing in his life became him like leaving it."
   (Malcolm in Act I, scene iv, lines 8–9)

4. "Yet do I fear thy nature. It is too full o' the milk of human kindness..."
   (Lady Macbeth in Act I, scene v, lines 14–15)

5. "Come, you spirits that tend on mortal thoughts, unsex me here..."
   (Lady Macbeth in Act I, scene v, lines 42–43)

6. "...look like the innocent flower, but be the serpent under it."
   (Lady Macbeth in Act I, scene v, lines 71–72)

7. "Will all great Neptune's ocean wash this blood clean from my hand?"
   (Macbeth in Act II, scene ii, lines 76–77)

Create, Exchange, Assess. In mathematics classrooms, this task involves groups in applying what they have learned by creating a mathematical problem that another group tries to solve. The group originating the problem then assesses their classmates' solution.

The task has a predictable structure:

- The teacher identifies the problem to be created (e.g., sketch a parabola that crosses the x-axis at two points and agree on a description for the parabola that could lead another group to replicate the graph).

- Groups each create a problem that meets the criteria.

- The teacher reviews and approves groups' work.

- Groups exchange problems with another group.

- Group members collaborate to solve the problem.

- When an exchanging pair of groups is ready, two members from one group trade places with two members from the other group, creating two mixed groups.

- In each new group, the two students who have stayed in place assess the work of the other group and encourage any necessary changes.

For example, in a lesson developing the concept of congruency, the teacher asks students in groups of four to draw two triangles and state the given congruent parts, making sure that what they state as "given," or what can be derived, is sufficient for proving the two triangles are congruent. The teacher reviews each group's work before it is exchanged with another group. The receiving group then writes the proof, and members of the originating group assess their solution. The teacher can follow up in the whole class as needed.

Literary Devices. After students have read a poem, short story, or novel, this task can extend their understanding by having them work in groups to identify excerpts from the text as representative of particular literary devices — for example, plot elements, elements in poetry, similes, metaphors, alliteration, and so on.

In the sample in figure 40, a class has read Shirley Jackson's story "The Lottery." Students each draw a card with a particular quote from the text, find the other classmates with the same quote, and work together to identify it as representative of one of six given plot elements, to define the literary term, and to explain how it is a good example of the term. The list of literary terms provided to all groups and the individual quotation cards that students draw are shown in figure 40.

Figure 40. Literary Devices Cards

The morning of June 27th was clear and sunny, with the fresh warmth of a full-summer day; the flowers were blossoming profusely and the grass was richly green.	Setting
Mr. Summers...was a round-faced, jovial man and he ran the coal business, and people were sorry for him because he had no children and his wife was a scold.	Character
Suddenly, Tessie Hutchinson shouted to Mr. Summers. "You didn't give him time enough to take any paper he wanted. I saw you. It wasn't fair!"	Conflict
"They do say," Mr. Adams said to Old Man Warner, who stood next to him, "that over in the north village they're talking of giving up the lottery." Old Man Warner snorted. "Pack of crazy fools," he said. "Listening to the young folks, nothing's good enough for them.	Motivation
"It's Tessie," Mr. Summers said, and his voice was hushed. "Show us her paper, Bill."	Climax
A stone hit her on the side of the head. Old Man Warner was saying, "Come on, come on, everyone."... And then they were upon her.	Resolution

Collaborative Dialogue Writing. In chapter 5, we saw groups of four in Roza Ng's class write and perform dialogues based on specific scenes from the Richard Wright text and connecting ideas in the text to their own experience. They followed the predictable structure of this task:

- The teacher identifies key scenes in a text.

- Different groups of four work with different scenes.

- Each group collaborates on a dialogue based on their scene;
  70 percent of the dialogue reflects evidence in the text, and
  30 percent reflects students' life experiences.

- Group members each make a copy of the group's dialogue.

- Groups practice their dialogue, providing each group member with
  a role in the performance.

- Groups perform their dialogues for the class.

We can see from the various tasks described above how tasks serve as scaffolding that focuses students on key ideas and allows them to practice, gain confidence, and appropriate (and modify) concepts, practices, and language. Over time, and as students develop expertise, the responsibility for scaffolds is "handed over," and students guide and support their own behavior, initially in conscious and explicit ways, which are eventually internalized and become mostly unconscious.

Conclusion

A teacher's invitations for students to engage in tasks that meet interrelated disciplinary, cognitive, and linguistic objectives will be as successful as the activities are powerful, are relevant, and serve real, important purposes. In this chapter we have looked at some of these ideas, discussing considerations that need to be applied to unit and lesson planning. Having observed or used these ideas with success in multiple classes, with many students who truly gained from and enjoyed them, we hope they provide a source of guidance and inspiration for our many colleagues who are trying to make the amazing potential of our students a reality.

Finally, we need to ask ourselves whether constructing lessons in ways described in this chapter and throughout the book is worth the effort and time that must be invested. We need to answer this question with a profound affirmative. Whenever as coaches or observers we have walked into the classrooms of teachers where students are invited to engage in verbal activity, risk making mistakes in the process, and finally feel the exhilaration of having conquered ideas, academic practices, and the language needed to communicate them all, we have witnessed the most powerful of educational experiences. All our students can excel if we ourselves work toward excellence. Even though we can never fully measure the results of our effort, we must trust that it extends in ways both broad and long-lasting — through the families, communities, and lifetimes of the students in our care.

REFERENCES

Agar, M. (1994). *Language shock: Understanding the culture of conversation.* New York: William Morrow.

Antón, M., & DiCamilla, F. (1988). Socio-cognitive functions of L1 collaborative interaction in the L2 classroom. *The Canadian Modern Language Review, 54*(3), 314–342.

Bakhurst, D. (1991). *Consciousness and revolution in Soviet psychology.* Cambridge, UK: Cambridge University Press.

Batalova, J., Fix, M., & Murray, J. (2007, March). *Measures of change: The demography and literacy of adolescent English learners: A report to Carnegie Corporation of New York.* Washington, DC: Migration Policy Institute.

Bransford, J., Brown, A., & Cocking, R. (Eds.). (2000). *How people learn: Brain, mind, experience, and school.* Washington, DC: National Academy Press.

Bransford, J., & Johnson, M. (1972). Contextual prerequisites for understanding: Some investigations of comprehension and recall. *Journal of Verbal Learning and Verbal Behavior, 11,* 717–726.

Bransford, J., & Johnson, M. (1973). Considerations of some problems of comprehension. In W. Chase (Ed.), *Visual information processing* (pp. 383–438). New York: Academic Press.

Bronfenbrenner, U. (1979). *The ecology of human development: Experiments by nature and design.* Cambridge, MA: Harvard University Press.

Brooks, F., Donato, R., & McGlone, J. (1997). When are they going to say 'it' right? Understanding learner talk during pair-work activity. *Foreign Language Annals, 30*(4), 524–541.

Bruner, J., & Sherwood, V. (1976). Peekaboo and the learning of rule structures. In J. Bruner, A. Jolly, & K. Sylva (Eds.), *Play: Its role in development and evolution* (pp. 277–87). Harmondsworth, UK: Penguin Books.

Cazden, C. (1981). Performance before competence: Assistance to child discourse in the zone of proximal development. *Quarterly Newsletter of the Laboratory of Comparative Human Cognition, 3,* 5–8.

Clay, M., & Cazden, C. (1992). A Vygotskian interpretation of Reading Recovery. In C. Cazden (Ed.), *Whole language plus: Essays on literacy in the United States and New Zealand* (pp. 114–135). New York: Teachers College Press.

Chomsky, N. (1986). *Knowledge of language.* Cambridge, MA: MIT Press.

Cohen, A., & Walqui, A. (2007). *Three moments in teaching a Robert Frost poem* [DVD]. San Francisco: WestEd.

Cohen, D. (1988). Teaching practice: Plus ça change .... In P. Jackson (Ed.), *Contributing to educational change: Perspectives on research and practice* (pp. 27–84). Richmond, CA: McCutchan Publishing.

Cole, M. (1985). The zone of proximal development: Where culture and cognition create each other. In J. Wertsch (Ed.), *Culture, communication, and cognition.* New York: Cambridge University Press.

Cook, V. (1995). Multi-competence and the learning of many languages. *Language, culture, and curriculum, 8*(2), 93–98.

Crescenzi, S., & Walqui, A. (2008). *Brain injury jigsaw project* [DVD]. San Francisco: WestEd.

Csikszentmihalyi, M. (1990). *Flow: The psychology of optimal experience.* New York: Harper and Row.

Csikszentmihalyi, M., & Schmidt, J. (1998). Stress and resilience in adolescence: An evolutionary perspective. In K. Borman & B. Schneider (Eds.), *The adolescent years: Social influences and educational challenges. Ninety-seventh Yearbook of the National Society for the Study of Education.* Chicago: The University of Chicago Press.

Cummins, J. (1984). *Bilingualism and special education: Issues in assessment and pedagogy.* San Diego, CA: College-Hill Press.

Cummins, J. (1996). *Negotiating identities: Education for empowerment in a diverse society.* Los Angeles: California Association for Bilingual Education.

Deci, E., & Flaste, R. (1995). *Why we do what we do: Understanding self-motivation.* New York: Penguin Group (USA).

DeFazio, A., & Walqui, A. (2001). *Where do you want to go next?* [DVD]. San Francisco: WestEd.

Donato, R. (1994). Collective scaffolding. In J. Lantolf & G. Appel (Eds.), *Vygotskian approaches to second language research* (pp. 33–56). Norwood, NJ: Ablex Publishers.

Ellis, R. (2005). *Instructed second language acquisition. A literature review.* Wellington, NZ: New Zealand Ministry of Education.

Ellis, R. (2006). Current issues in the teaching of grammar: An SLA perspective. *TESOL Quarterly, 40*(1), 83–107.

Ellis, R. (2008). Principles of instructed second language acquisition. *CAL Digest,* Washington, DC: Center for Applied Linguistics.

Elmore, R. F. (1996). Getting to scale with good educational practices. *Harvard Educational Review, 66,* 1–25.

Fleming, S. (1994). *It takes two to tango.* Unpublished MA project, Monterey Institute of International Studies, Monterey, CA.

Frost, R. (1916). The road not taken. Retrieved April 15, 2009, from http://en.wikipedia.org/wiki/The_Road_Not_Taken_(poem)

Gándara, P., & Contreras, F. (2009). *The Latino education crisis. The consequences of failed social policies.* Cambridge, MA: Harvard University Press.

Gándara, P., Maxwell-Jolly, J., & Driscoll, A. (2005). *Listening to teachers of English language learners: A survey of California teachers' challenges, experiences, and professional development needs.* Santa Cruz, CA: The Center for the Future of Teaching and Learning.

García, V., Agbemakplido, W., Abdella, H., Lopez, O., & Registe, R. (2006). High school students' perspectives on the 2001 No Child Left Behind Act's definition of a highly qualified teacher. *Harvard Educational Review, 76*(4), 698–724.

Gibbons, P. (2002). *Scaffolding language, scaffolding learning.* Portsmouth, NH: Heinemann.

Gibbons, P. (2003). Mediating language learning: Teacher interactions with ESL students in a content based classroom. *TESOL Quarterly, 37*(2), 247–273.

Gibbons, P. (2005). Putting scaffolding to work: The contribution of scaffolding in articulating ESL education. *Prospect, 20*(1), 6–30.

Gibbons, P. (2009). *English learners, academic literacy, and thinking: Learning in the challenge zone.* Portsmouth, NH: Heinemann.

Gibbs, R. (2005). *Embodiment and cognitive science.* New York: Cambridge University Press.

Gonzales, A., & Walqui, A. (2004). *Appropriating the academic language of geometry* [DVD]. San Francisco: WestEd.

Graves, K. (1996). A framework of course development processes. In K. Graves (Ed.), *Teachers as course developers* (pp. 12–38). Cambridge, UK: Cambridge University Press.

Hernandez, A. (n.d.). Second-language writers: The writing of second-language children. In *Professional development for teachers of English language learners.* San Diego, CA: San Diego County Office of Education.

Hopstock, P., & Stephenson, T. (2003). *Descriptive study of services to LEP students and LEP students with disabilities. Special topic report #2: Analysis of Office of Civil Rights (OCR) data related to LEP students.* Washington, DC: U.S. Department of Education, Office of English Language Acquisition, Language Enhancement, and Academic Achievement for Limited English Proficient Students (OELA).

Jastrow, J. (1899). The mind's eye. *Popular Science Monthly, 54,* 299–312. Retrieved April 2, 2009, from http://commons.wikimedia.org/wiki/File:Duck-Rabbit_illusion.jpg

Kramsch, C. (1993). *Context and culture in language teaching.* Oxford, UK: Oxford University Press.

Lantolf, J., & Thorne, S. (2006). *Sociocultural theory and the genesis of second language development.* Oxford, UK: Oxford University Press.

Lave, J., & Wenger, E. (1991). *Situated learning: Legitimate peripheral participation.* New York: Cambridge University Press.

Long, M. (1996). The role of linguistic environment in second language acquisition. In W. Ritchie & T. Bhatia (Eds.), *Handbook of second language acquisition* (pp. 413–468). San Diego, CA: Academic Press.

Mercer, N. (1995). *The guided construction of knowledge: Talk between teachers and learners in the classroom.* Clevedon, UK: Multilingual Matters.

Merton, R. (1968). *Social theory and social structure* (Rev. ed.). New York: The Free Press.

Ng, R., & Walqui, A. (2005a). *Teaching* Black Boy *in three moments* [DVD]. San Francisco: WestEd.

Ng, R., & Walqui, A. (2005b). *Oral development jigsaw project* [DVD]. San Francisco: WestEd.

Norton Peirce, B. (1995). Social identity, investment, and language learning. *TESOL Quarterly, 29*(1), 9–31.

Passel, J. (2006, March 7). The size and characteristics of the unauthorized migrant population in the U.S. *PEW Hispanic Center*. Retrieved October 10, 2009, from http://pewhispanic.org/reports/report.php?ReportID = 61

Pinker, S. (1994). *The language instinct*. New York: William Morrow.

Price, J., & Walqui, A. (2001). *Scaffolding the 14th Amendment* [DVD]. San Francisco: WestEd.

Quality Teaching for English Learners. (2006). Unit 3: Introduction to Shakespeare: *Macbeth. Module 10. Teaching language arts 11–12 to English language learners*. San Francisco: WestEd.

Resnick, L., Hall, M., & Fellows of the Institute for Learning. (2006). *Principles of learning: Study tools for education* [CD-ROM]. Pittsburgh, PA: University of Pittsburgh, Institute for Learning, Learning Research and Development Center.

Rodríguez, Luis. (1993). *Always running: La vida loca: Gang days in L.A.* New York: Touchstone.

Rogoff, B. (1995). Observing sociocultural activity on three planes: Participatory appropriation, guided participation, and apprenticeship. In J. Wertsch, P. del Rio, & A. Alvarez (Eds.), *Sociocultural studies of the mind* (pp. 139–164). New York: Cambridge University Press.

Rosenthal, R., & Jacobson, L. (1966). Teachers' expectancies: Determinates of pupils' IQ gains. *Psychological Reports, 19,* 115–118.

Ryan, K., & Walqui, A. (2008). *Novel ideas only in preparing learners to read "The Necklace"* [DVD]. San Francisco: WestEd.

Schleppegrell, M. (forthcoming). *Language in academic subject areas and classroom instruction: What is academic language and how can we teach it?*

Shakespeare, W. (n.d.). *Macbeth.* Retrieved April 15, 2009, from http://www.gutenberg.org/etext/2264

Shulman, L. (1987). Knowledge and teaching: Foundations of the new reform. *Harvard Educational Review, 57,* 114–35.

Skutnabb-Kangas, T. (1984). *Bilingualism or not: The education of minorities.* Clevedon, UK: Multilingual Matters.

Stenhouse, L. (1975). *An introduction to curriculum research and development.* London: Heinneman.

Suárez-Orozco, C., Suárez-Orozco, M., & Todorova, I. (2008). Learning a new land. Immigrant students in American society. Cambridge, MA: The Belknap Press of Harvard University Press.

Swain, M., & Lapkin, S. (2000). Task-based second language learning: The uses of the first language. *Language Teaching Research, 4*(3), 251–274.

Tharp, R., & Gallimore, R. (1988). *Rousing minds to life: Teaching, learning, and schooling in social context.* New York: Cambridge University Press.

Turnbull, M., & Arnett, K. (2002). Teachers' uses of the target and first languages in second and foreign language classrooms. *Annual Review of Applied Linguistics, 22,* 204–218.

Valsiner, J. (2006, September). *Beyond the first language: Acquisition without learning.* Invited presentation at the Thirteenth Annual Sociocultural Theory and Second Language Learning Research Working Group, University of Massachusetts, Amherst.

van Lier, L. (1996). *Interaction in the language curriculum: Awareness, autonomy, and authenticity.* London: Longman.

van Lier, L. (2004). *The ecology and semiotics of language learning: A socio-cultural perspective.* Dordrecht, NL: Kluwer Academic.

Verhoeven, L. (1990). Acquisition of reading in a second language. *Reading Research Quarterly, 25,* 90–114.

Voloshinov, V. (1973). *Marxism and the philosophy of language.* Cambridge, MA: Harvard University Press.

Vygotsky, L. (1962). *Thought and language.* Cambridge, MA: MIT Press.

Vygotsky, L. (1976). Play and its role in the mental development of the child. In J. Bruner, A. Jolly, & K. Sylva (Eds.), *Play: Its role in development and evolution* (pp. 537–554). Harmondsworth, UK: Penguin Books.

Vygotsky, L. (1978). *Mind in society.* Cambridge, MA: Harvard University Press.

Walqui, A. (1992). *Sheltered instruction: Doing it right.* San Diego, CA. San Diego County Office of Education.

Walqui, A. (2001). Accomplished teaching with English learners: A conceptualization of teacher expertise. *Multilingual Educator 1*(4), 55–55.

Wood, D., Bruner, J., & Ross, G. (1976). The role of tutoring in problem solving. *Journal of Child Psychology and Psychiatry, 17,* 89–100.

Wright, R. (1945/1998). *Black Boy.* New York: HarperCollins.

APPENDIX
Linguistics in the ELL Classroom

Anthony J. DeFazio

International High School at La Guardia Community College

It may seem counterintuitive, at first glance, to use linguistics as subject matter content for high school English language learners. After all, theoretical linguistics is abstract. The language used to explain its concepts is dense and difficult even for many native speakers. In addition, it is difficult to find readable and interesting material on the subject that is accessible to high school students. These are all sensible objections. However, I would argue that the advantages obtained by using linguistics as a theme with English language learners outweighs the disadvantages.

Why Linguistics?

Focusing on language in the guise of linguistics can be profitable both for students and teacher if we embrace certain guidelines:

- First, examine linguistics in a comparative sense.

- Second, build in appropriate scaffolds, especially when using difficult readings and when analyzing difficult structures.

- Third, encourage students to work both in same language groups and different language groups, depending on the nature of the material being studied.

- Fourth, find some way to connect the study of language with the students' own lives.

- Finally, capitalize on the interdisciplinary nature of linguistics to reach students who don't think they enjoy language study.

Linguistics offers the ESL teacher an opportunity to focus on form, yet still maintain an emphasis on communication, collaboration, and classroom interactions. My students and I can investigate form by examining the ways that the various languages in the class construct any one of a number of structures — passivization, question formation, relative clause formation, for example — and then comparing these with English. Using linguistics as a subject matter also helps students revisit their intuitions regarding the grammars of their first language. When students work in same language groups to examine structures in the first language, they are often astounded by what they find. Time and time again I hear the refrain, "I didn't know we did that in my language." Students who tell me, at the beginning of the term, that their language has no grammar soon become amazed at the complexities they find.

There are other rationales for using linguistics as a content subject matter.* They can be summarized as follows:

- Linguistics builds on what students already know. Cummins (2000) suggests that we draw on students' own expertise, on their prior knowledge to facilitate learning. It follows that we should use material that students relate to. Comparative linguistics is one such field. It builds on the L1 knowledge of students. It draws on their experiences and intuitions with their first language, yet it forces them to look at this material in a new way since students may

---

* Of course, other subject matter can provide many of these same benefits; yet linguistics is the only one that seems to accommodate *all* of these benefits.

never have thought of their first language as an object of inquiry, let alone an object of inquiry in an empirical sense.

- Brand new students to the class, who have not yet learned much English, can contribute to the class work — in their own language and with the help of their more English-fluent classmates. These new students can feel as if they are a valuable part of the classroom activities since they can offer insights and examples too, even if they are not yet able to communicate in English.

- Linguistics, as a subject matter, allows the class to focus on form, maintain an emphasis on communication, and still allow for teacher-directed lessons, when required. Anton (1999) explains how trends in learner-centeredness have often been interpreted to mean pair and group work with the teacher's role missing. She describes classrooms which still maintain a student-centered atmosphere but where "teacher-learner exchanges...lead learners to become highly involved in the negotiation of meaning and linguistic form." The class I am describing here is, I hope, one example of the kind of classroom she is describing.

- Studying linguistics can help students to see the disparity between their own learning and the requirements of the target language (Schmidt, 1990). Rutherford and Smith (1988) might argue that it might lead to consciousness raising on the part of students.

- The content matter of linguistics puts the teacher in the role of learner in a meaningful way since many of the structures students analyze, the questions they bring, and the intuitions they have may not be readily available to the instructor. He/she will have to research answers to many questions in a comparative linguistics class and may no longer have the answer to all the questions posed. This models lifetime learning at its best.

- Linguistics is an inherently fascinating subject, not only in its own right, but also in its interdisciplinary applications. Students are attracted to questions related to language. With linguistics as a focus, students can make connections with physics (phonetics, hearing, sound), with computer science (computer languages, translation), with biology and psychology (animal communication systems, learning theory) with philosophy (the nature of thinking), with social issues (dialect, the development of AAVE), standard language, language and power, language and gender). Students can also explore traditional grammar conventions, research their history, and explore when and if they diverge from linguistic theory.

Theoretical linguistics is, of course, a vast subject, and working within a comparative framework is daunting even for a trained linguist. I have come to rely on several texts to help me. Bernard Comrie's *The World's Major Languages* is a technical introduction to many of the structures students will research. David Crystal's *The Encyclopedia of Language* is also helpful in offering a comprehensive overview of the field. Leo van Lier's excellent *Introducing Language Awareness* is extremely helpful since it is written in an accessible and entertaining style, one that welcomes students and teachers into language investigation. *Linguistics for Humans* by Cari Springer has also proven beneficial since its explanations are accessible to the novice linguist. Apart from these last two texts, the majority of material for students will probably need to be written by the instructor. If the course continues to be taught, the students themselves can become authors of some of the material that later groups of students will use to grapple with the complexities of the field.

How Linguistics Fits at International High School

I first became interested in this subject as a graduate student in theoretical linguistics at New York University, but later switched to TESOL/Second Language Learning. I have tried to keep up with the field through various linguistics institutes both here and abroad, but soon realized that having the latest incarnation of generative grammar or whatever was in ascendancy was not as important as introducing the students into the beauty and complexity of language as an object of investigation. I teach at the International High School in New York City, a small (about 450 students) school for immigrant students. International's students come from over fifty countries and speak over forty languages. The predominant language groups (2002) are Spanish, Mandarin, Polish, Bengali, Portuguese, Korean, and Arabic. To enter the school — which serves only English language learners and offers a complete high school education including external internships in the workplace — students need to score below the 20th percentile on a test of English language proficiency and have been in the United States less than four years at time of entry. Many students have been in the United States less than a year when they enter International. Over three-quarters of the students are eligible for federally mandated free lunch programs based on their family's per-capita income. International's students belong to the category referred to as "high-risk" students, at least in part because they have not yet mastered English and because students who fit their profile often have a high dropout rate. Our graduation rate has remained steady at over 90 percent.

The school has a formal mission statement that limns its approach to education and the role of language in learning. Specifically, the school maintains that

- language is the key to learning; proficiency in academic language emerges most naturally in experiential, language-rich interdisciplinary study;

- fluency in two languages is a resource for the student and for the community;

- students learn best from each other in heterogeneous, collaborative groups;

- learning is facilitated when collaboration exists between the school, home, and the community at large;

- assessment must support individual growth; there must be a variety of opportunities for students and faculty to demonstrate what they can do. (Cummins, 2000, p. 158)

Teachers are grouped into six academic teams, each with its own guidance counselor. Three of the school's teams work with students in their first two years of high school, three with students who are in their last two years. The teams were originally designed as interdisciplinary learning communities, but the thematic ties have loosened somewhat owing to state-mandated exit examinations. The present teams are *Origins, American Dream, Connections, World Around Us, Project and Adventures in New York City,* and *Inquiry and Action.* Students stay with the same group of teachers for two years and then move up. There is no attempt to segregate students on the basis of their English language knowledge; beginning students and students who are at least on the intermediate level sit side by side in the junior institute.

Themes in Linguistics Unit of Study

I have been with the *Origins* team as a humanities teacher for almost six years. During this time, I have spent a large part of each year teaching sheltered world history, with some attention to literature. Each spring, however, I would devote several weeks to linguistics. While the specific topics vary from year to year, here is a thumbnail sketch of the themes this linguistics curriculum explores and how students interact with the material.

Theme 1: What is language?

Students work in small mixed language groups to create semantic maps (learning webs) of the question What is language? I usually have four or five leading questions (e.g., How many languages are there in the world? How do a first and second language compare?) that I use to focus students' attention to key concepts. Students are asked to translate the word *language* into all the languages of their group and to arrive at no fewer than twenty different items that could be used to explain the term. Some students choose to read from encyclopedia articles and books, and to undertake Internet research to arrive at a response to this question. Others choose to arrive at a response only from the information the students bring to the group. The semantic maps, once finished, are mounted and each group presents and explains the material outlined on the learning web (see sample semantic maps 1 and 2 below). Students can then revise their learning webs based on the information they have heard others present. Here are the semantic maps of two different groups. They show how two groups of students at varying levels of English proficiency developed their response to the topic, *What is language?*

To demonstrate what they have learned, students write the first of a series of personal letters on the subject, the letters to be collected in a book each student produces called *What Is Language?* Each student will create his/her own book even though much of the information they uncover is arrived at collaboratively. Originally, students wrote formal academic essays, but I abandoned this idea in an effort to eliminate plagiarism and to increase the level of student voice in the essays. I also wanted the writing to be more interesting to read for the students, and the epistolary form seemed a good compromise. The letter has a formal structure that is easy to model, yet it provides students with a form to explore a topic at any depth they wish. The letters can be both humorous and academic at the same time. Students are encouraged to write to anyone whom they think might be interested

Semantic Map 1

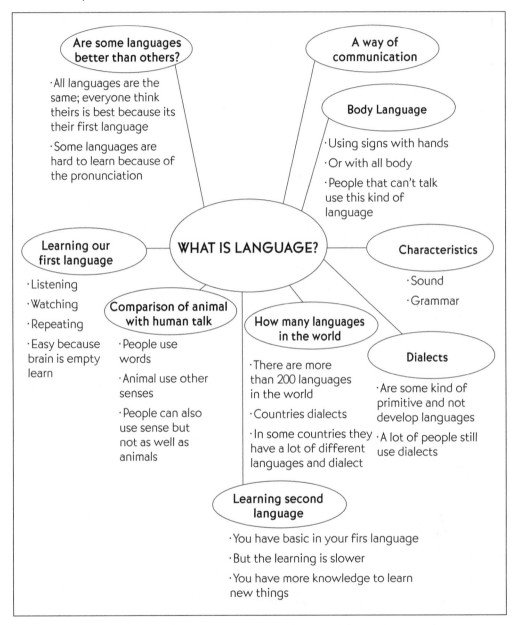

Semantic Map 2

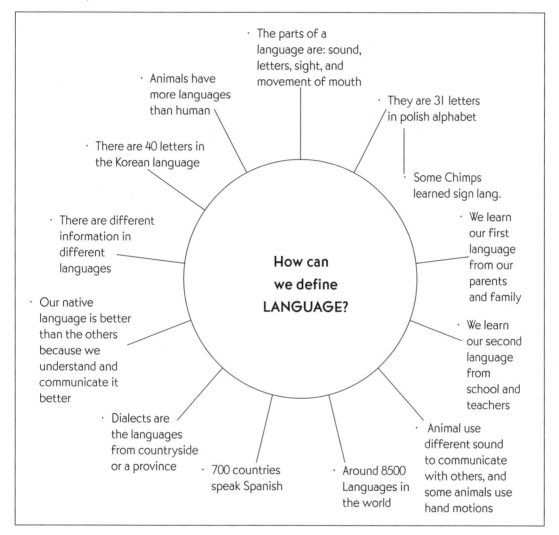

in learning about linguistics and, equally important, about what they are doing in school. Some of the people students chose to address seemed strange to me, but students had good reasons for the people they chose to write to. Here is a part of one student's letter. The letters are unedited.

Dear Alexander,

How have you been? How are you going in the school? How is your family? I hope that you and the family are ok and that you are getting good grades in school. Now I would like to let you know what I'm learning in humanities because the project we have begun now seems to be interesting. It is about linguistics and will take us up to 5 weeks to finish it. Each week we will learning a different topic; the topic for this week is How do we know that something is a language? TO answer this question I had to research about language, its characteristic and animal communication. According to my research. I found out that there are more than 6,500 different languages and between 7,000 and 8,000 dialects, where many of them are on their way to disappearing...

Here is an example from a less fluent writer of English; what this writer lacks in linguistic grace, however, she makes up for in her content. She chose to write to Alex Rodriguez, the baseball player.

Dear: Alex Rodriguez,

I hope that you and your family are ok. How you feeling? How you doing in work? I saw you playing baseball this Saturday and I really prod of you. Ok, I wrote this letter to tell you what we are learning in the school. This class we learning about language. Language is the way to express what you feeling like in body language. grammar, sign language, vocabulary, alphabet, sounds and pronunciation. Yesterday we spoke what we had learned over this research we find out that the language that is more spoken in the entire world is Chinese. The second language is English and the third is Spanish. So we need to be proud that we speak two languages.

I know it was not hard for you to speak both languages because you were born here with your mother who spoke Spanish. I have a question for you; do you know how you learn your first language? Ok these is my opinion. I think when you are a baby you listen to your parents, TV and other person speaking over and over that you copy what they say without knowing what it means. The second language is harder because you already know how to speak your first language and is hard to make some pronunciation and also you are trying to compare your first language...I have another question for you; is animal communication language? I know this question is hard to understand but it is a language. You see bees use dance to tell other bees were they found the nectar to produce the honey and like that talk to one another...

Theme 2: Sounds

This topic focuses on the sounds found in the world's languages.

We usually begin by looking at lists of words. Students are asked to determine the number of sounds and syllables in words ranging from simple ones like *house* to more complex words such as *pterodactyl*. They often ask me to keep pronouncing the more unusual words. This leads to a discussion of sounds, silent letters, and spelling in English and segues nicely into the International Phonetic Alphabet and its importance in linguistics. I used a simplified version of the alphabet adapted from the Ohio University Language Files. We discuss the nature of consonants, vowels, and diphthongs. We practice the sounds on the IPA orally, after I explain how and where consonants, vowels, and diphthongs are made in the human vocal tract. I introduce the idea of transcription and ask students to write transcriptions of words in English and their native languages. The fun begins when we go to the chalkboard and challenge one another to write the sounds in the languages in the class. I improvise a phonetic symbol if the students have a sound in their language we do not have IPA equivalent for. We also practice tongue twisters in the languages of the class. This lesson, like all the others, ends with a letter students write about "The Sounds of English and My First Language." Students explain the IPA, transcription, and sounds that they find difficult to make in English.

Theme 3: Syntax

We begin by looking at the lexical categories linguists generally explore. I give students lists of words that I identify as nouns, verbs, adjectives, and prepositions, and I then ask them to figure out what they have in common.

Often the discussion concentrates on semantic considerations as the distinguishing feature for lexical categories. Students, for example, have often heard the statement that nouns are names of persons, places, and things. My role becomes one of opening up the definition to include syntactic considerations. I introduce phrase structure diagrams using a simplified version, drawn from a very early version of transformation grammar, circa 1957. Students spend time — in small groups — trying to figure out how to draw trees of various kinds of sentences. I ask them to compare sentences in English with their first language and to draw trees of both sentences. I usually develop the system up to relative clause formation, though some students never get that far and stay with the simple sentence. We discuss verb valence and how a verb gets the arguments it requires and how this information is manifested in the phrase structure trees we create. As always, the lesson ends with the students writing a chapter in their linguistics book on a comparison of syntax in their first language and in English. Here is a sample of one student's letter about syntax:

Dear Mr. DeFazio:

Annyounghaseyo! (which means Hi in Korean but in more honorific expression). 8 months had already passed since I came to this class and study under your honorable teaching. During the last 8 months, my English skills were able to improve a lot since you pushed us to do more and harder works. I really like the way you teach us. They really helped me to challenge myself to new things. I often found myself working harder and harder. Thank you. Anyway, I better stop adulating and get to the point.

Syntax was very interesting. I really loved learning about the syntax, although I was confused a lot. Umm. Sentence is divided into two parts: NP and VP. Some of the lexical categories in NP are noun, pronoun, determiners while VP can be divided into tense and verb. Sometimes PP (prepositional phrase) can be in the VP. However, if the sentence contains a conjunctive word such as and, while, but the sentence has to be divided into three parts. For example, *A boy cried when he fell down from the stair.* A boy cried is one sentence and from when to the stair is another sentence. Therefore, when we make a tree of this sentence, there should be two S in the tree, like this:

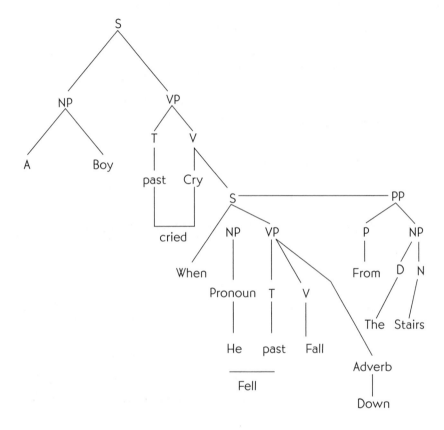

Well, I think it will be the last paragraph of this letter. I enjoyed learning about syntax. I think you were right. It is like mathematics. All those lexical categories make up a sentence, just like in mathematics. You divided the sentence into different parts. And when you add them, they'll make up a sentences.

Sincerely,
Eric L.

Theme 4

The last topic in the linguistics program varies from semester to semester, depending on the interests of the students. Sometimes, as during the controversy about African American Vernacular English and bilingual education/ English only movement, I decide to focus on one topic that has political or social importance. At other times, I have given students *carte blanche* to initiate their own projects and research. The only stipulation is that students work in collaborative groups and write another letter in their books to explain their findings. There have been a variety of projects, among them

- Children's books on language

- Dialect studies of the students' home countries

- What kind of syntax do the teachers at the International High School use?

- Which teacher has the most complicated speech and why

- What do our teachers know about grammar and linguistics?

For many of these research projects students became field linguists. They taped, transcribed, and analyzed. Often they developed graphical representations of what they found, as when they explored the number of complex sentence patterns exhibited by different teachers at International.

Approaches to the Unit Instruction

Without doubt, the material students study in linguistics is difficult both conceptually and linguistically. But that is no reason to shy away from it. We do not shy away from world history or science, material with equally difficult reading for second language learners. Students welcome the challenge of exploring language from an empirical point of view, and they can be successful provided we supply certain supports to help them.

First, I introduce most units with some kind of student activity — semantic map, hands-on activity, questionnaire — to see what students already know about the subject. Direct lecture with appropriate second language methodology is then used to introduce additional material.

Second, a great deal of practice is built into all of the activities. I use a variety of reading and writing activities, and I build in substantial student choice to allow students to explore the material introduced in the readings and lectures. Consider syntax, for example. I often give lists of sentences graded in difficulty, ranging from "Everyone can do these" to "These will challenge the graduate students among you." Students are encouraged to work in collaborative groups to complete the analyses.

Third, native language use is encouraged to help students understand the material they are working on. It is also used to help students who are new to the class feel they are a part of the material, although this presupposes that with beginning students there is someone in the class who speaks the student's language. When first language assistance is not available, then I seek resources outside of the classroom, often a student with a free period or a paraprofessional.

Fourth, varied assessments are used to evaluate student work. I do not expect all students to end up at the same place. I occasionally use tests — in addition to the portfolio model of assessment — but the tests are often collaborative. For instance, I'll ask groups of students to take up a question such as Why did the chicken cross the street? Students are asked to write the sentence in phonetic script and then answer the question using phonetic script. I will ask them to draw trees of sentences at varying levels of difficulty so that their total number of points adds up to 50. In this way, a student can do five easy questions and no difficult questions. To those who ask if I am giving students an easy way out with this kind of testing,

I would respond (1) the material is difficult enough in English, let alone when a student is using English as a second language; (2) I trust students enough to challenge themselves; and (3) the collaborative nature of the test encourages students to try more difficult sentences. Furthermore, testing is only one of the many assessments I use.

Fifth, the material is challenging. Students are expected to perform at a high level, but a level that is consonant with their English language level. I do not expect that all students will end up with the same information packaged in the same way. But I do expect that they will have moved significantly from where they started.

In the future, I will be teaching an elective, semester-long class in linguistics to English language learners. I will expand on the mentioned topics and include morphology and phonology as well. I plan to introduce problem sets to bring the level of analysis and difficulty up a notch. I am also negotiating to have experts on various language families work with me in class to deepen the analysis of the native languages we carry out in our research. I hope this further demonstrates that learning is ongoing, that collaboration is often essential, and that the study of linguistics remains a challenging cognitive activity with questions to be explored. I want to invite students into that exploration and get them to see that their bilingualism is an asset, not a deficiency, in their academic quest.

References

Anton, M. (1999). The discourse of a learner-centered classroom: Sociocultural perspectives on teacher-centered interaction in the second language classroom. *Modern Language Journal, 83*(3) 303–318.

Comrie, B. (Ed.). (1990). *The world's major languages.* New York: Oxford University Press.

Crystal, D. (1987). *The Cambridge encyclopedia of language*. New York: Cambridge University Press.

Cummins, J. (2000). *Language, power, and pedagogy*. Buffalo, NY: Multilingual Matters.

Jannedy, S., Poletto, R., & Weldon, T. (1994). *Language files*. Columbus: Ohio State University Press.

Rutherford, W., & Sharwood Smith, M. (1988). *Grammar and second language teaching*. New York: Newbury House.

Schmidt, R. (1990). The role of consciousness-raising in second language learning. *Applied Linguistics, 11*(2), 129–158.

Schmidt, R. (1992). Awareness and second language acquisition. *Annual Review of Applied Linguistics, 13,* 206–226.

Spring, C. (1997). *Linguistics for humans: A little book of basics*. Catalina, AZ: Real Grammar.

Spring, C. (1997). *Linguistics for humans: Field-based learning exercises*. Catalina, AZ: Real Grammar.

van Lier, L. (1995). *Introducing language awareness*. New York: Penguin.

INDEX

cognition, cognitive psychology, 4–6
Cognitive Academic Language
  Proficiency (CALP), 46
cognitive complexity, 46
cognitive skills (higher-order thinking)
  development, 82–84, 87, 132, 143–144
collaborative dialogue writing tasks,
  110, 115–117, 132–133, 152–153,
  178, 185
collaborative posters, 35
collaborative scaffolding, 30
competition among languages, 58–59
complexity, 46, 71
content topics, 144–145
contingency, 34, 37
continuity, coherence, 34–35
conversational language, 45–51. *See also*
  playground language
Cook, Vivian, 59
create, exchange, assess task, 182–183
Crescenzi, Stacia, 104–107, 119–137
cricket (game), 63, 75–76
Cummins, Jim, 44, 46
curriculum. *See* quality curriculum

DeFazio, Tony, 40, 50, 94–97, 143–151,
  199–214
degrees of freedom, 21, 38
designing instruction, 139–186
developmental psychology, 7
dialectical journal. *See* double-entry
  journal tasks
dialogical language use, 7, 19, 23
dialogue performance tasks, 153
DiCamilla, Fred, 59–60
differentiation, 88–93
disciplinary knowledge, 86, 144
disciplinary language, 85, 145. *See also*
  subject matter language
discourse, 66–67
diversity in the classroom, 1, 11

Donato, Richard, 29, 56
double-entry journal tasks
  described, 2–4
  in *Black Boy* study, 169–171
  in brain-injury study, 135
  in "Hunger" study, 152–153
  in interacting with text moment, 153,
    169
  in *Macbeth* study, 170–171
  promoting literary characterization
    skills, 110, 113–115, 118

Elmore, Richard, 86
emergence (handover/takeover), 34, 37
everyday language. *See* conversational
  language
expectations. *See* high expectations
  for students
expected, unexpected events. *See*
  unpredictable vs. predictable outcomes
experimentation, student, 31
expert group discussion, writing,
  reading tasks, 91, 121, 124–128, 134
expert-novice interactions, 28–33, 40–41
extended anticipatory guide tasks, 123,
  155, 165–167. *See also* anticipatory
  guide tasks
extending understanding. *See* three
  moments in a lesson
extralinguistic contexts, 39–40. *See also*
  non-linguistic meaning elements
extralinguistic meaning elements, 66-67

famous phrases tasks, 181–182
feedback, 73–76. See also assessments
first-generation English language
  learners, 104–105, 154. *See also*
  second-generation English language
  learners
Fleming, Siobhan, 61
flow, 34, 36

round-robin tasks, 35, 110–111, 121–122, 135, 152–153, 155, 157–159

rubrics, 84, 92–93. *See also* mind-mirror rubric tasks

rule-bound game elements, 18

SLA. *See* Second Language Acquisition

scaffolding. *See also* three moments in a lesson

overview, 15–41

defined, 12, 24

in classrooms, 23–40

collaborative, 30

expert-novice interactions, 28–33, 40–41

features of, 33–38

goals and, 20–21, 77

high expectations supported by, 84, 90

linguistic, 199

pedagogical, 33–40

in the peekaboo game, 18–19, 22, 25

purposes, 25

schema assisted by, 64

six essential elements of, 21–22

student-guided, 185

teachers' goals and, 107

tutoring setting of, 20–22

ZPD interaction, 15

schema, 62–66, 76–77, 158, 171

Schleppegrell, Mary, 49–51

script, scripts, 62–63, 110, 115–117, 135, 153, 213

second-generation English language learners, 104–105, 119, 129–131, 154. *See also* first-generation English language learners

Second Language Acquisition (SLA), 28–29

self-fulfilling prophecies, 88

Shakespeare, William. *See Macbeth* study unit

Sherwood, Virginia, 18–19

simplification, 21, 38–41, 85, 97, 135. *See also* amplification

Sizer, Ted, 87

social interaction, 7–8, 16, 132, 168

Social Theory and Social Structure (Merton), 88

sociocultural learning theory, 4–12

sociolinguistics, 4–5

spelling, 74, 98–99, 127, 209

spiraling progressions, 85, 99

Stenhouse, Lawrence, 24–25

structure. *See* scaffolding

style shifting, 50, 147

subject matter language, 44. *See also* disciplinary language

summative assessment, feedback, 75–76

supportive environments, 25, 34–36, 50, 146

supportive structures, 15, 25

Swain, Merrill, 71–73

takeover. *See* handover/takeover

tasks

defined, 107–108

anticipatory guide, 121, 155, 163–165

base group comparing/sharing, 91, 121, 125, 127–130, 133–135, 161–162

brain structure/function understood via, 119–131

clarifying bookmark/partner clarifying bookmark, 169, 173–175

collaborative dialogue writing, 110, 115–117, 132–133, 152–153, 178, 185

create, exchange, assess, 182–183

dialogue performance, 153

ABOUT THE AUTHORS

Aída Walqui, a native of Peru, first came to the United States as a college student, earning a BA at Connecticut College. As a Fulbright scholar, she received an MA in sociolinguistics from Georgetown University. Later in her career, she earned a PhD at Stanford University. Intervening experiences found her teaching in rural Andean communities; at universities in Mexico, the United Kingdom, and the United States; and in high school classrooms in Salinas, California. At WestEd, Walqui directs the Teacher Professional Development Program as well as QTEL, and consults nationally and internationally.

Leo van Lier was born in The Netherlands, where he began his teaching career. He later received his PhD in linguistics from Lancaster University in the United Kingdom and worked and taught in Europe, Latin America, and Asia, as well as in the United States. van Lier made a lasting contribution to second-language teaching theory, research, and practice because he never sought to sharply differentiate these worlds. Starting with his seminal 1988 book *The Classroom and the Language Learner: Ethnography and Second-Language Classroom Research* (Longman), and throughout his many other publications, van Lier presented an ecological view of language learning where negotiated interaction is central — on the one hand among persons within an environment and on the other *between* such persons *and* that enveloping environment. At the time of his death in 2012, he was Professor of Educational Linguistics in the Graduate School of Translation, Interpretation, and Language Education at the Monterey Institute of International Studies.

QTEL Services and Technical Assistance

What is Quality Teaching for English Learners (QTEL)?

WestEd's Quality Teaching for English Learners (QTEL) is a unique professional development program that helps teachers and teacher educators become better equipped to educate secondary students who are also learning English as a second language. It offers theoretical and practical strategies for effectively teaching the academic language, conceptual understandings, and skills that are critical to ensuring that English language learners are fully prepared to benefit from education.

Instead of simplifying the curriculum and lowering expectations for English language learners, QTEL offers an academic framework rich in intellectual challenge along with high levels of support. The QTEL approach of providing high-challenge, high-support learning opportunities develops teacher expertise and raises student achievement. Academically rigorous though it is, teachers find the QTEL approach classroom friendly and pragmatic. Because it is grounded in sociocultural learning theory, teachers experience QTEL as a coherent, compelling way to work with students. They learn concrete ways to challenge and support their English language learners — and they understand why those strategies make sense.

Principles of Success

Five principles guide QTEL's work with and on behalf of teachers and students:

- Sustain academic rigor
- Hold high expectations
- Engage in high-quality teacher and student interactions
- Sustain a language focus
- Develop a high-quality curriculum

These principles reflect the QTEL belief that teacher and student development is a consequence of carefully planned opportunities to participate in meaningful and demanding academic activity with others.

Customized Professional Development

WestEd offers Quality Teaching for English Learners (QTEL) services in a variety of formats to meet your needs.

Capacity Building

In partnership with schools and districts, QTEL designs professional development that ranges from districtwide implementation to intensive work with whole schools and classroom coaching of individual teachers. An option to certify local staff developers to sustain and expand QTEL implementation is also available.

Professional Development Certification

Districts and schools that undertake a three-year QTEL implementation have the option of designating local staff to train specifically to become QTEL professional developers, certified to sustain and expand local QTEL implementation.

Open Enrollment Summer Institutes

Teacher Institutes

QTEL offers five-day intensive summer institutes for teachers in literacy as well as institutes for teachers in the content areas.

Leadership Institutes

QTEL offers five-day summer institutes for principals, assistant principals, and curriculum coordinators to complement the teacher institutes.

Contact Us

For more information, visit WestEd.org/qtel.